THE CHURCH OF ENGLAND
AND THE
ECUMENICAL MOVEMENT

THE

CHURCH OF ENGLAND

AND THE

ECUMENICAL MOVEMENT

by

The Reverend

JAMES GOOD, D.D., Ph.D.

Professor of Theology,
University College, Cork

CORK UNIVERSITY PRESS
BURNS & OATES · LONDON
1961

NIHIL OBSTAT :

JEREMIAH J. O'SULLIVAN, D.D.,
Censor Deputatus,

29 December, 1960.

IMPRIMATUR :

✠ CORNELIUS,
Episcopus Corcag. et Ross.
23/1/1961.

MADE AND PRINTED IN THE REPUBLIC OF IRELAND

CONTENTS

INTRODUCTION

In January of the year 1959 Pope John XXIII announced his intention of calling an Ecumenical Council of the Catholic Church. In succeeding months the word Ecumenical became commonplace with the average Catholic; he was told that the word Ecumenical meant simply 'world-wide'; he gradually learned the reasons for the calling of the Council, and heard at least a little about the great Councils of the past. At the same time he became aware that the word had been in common usage among our non-Catholic brethren for the last half-century, being used to describe a great international movement to achieve unity among the separated churches. It is about this world-wide movement towards Christian reunion that this book is written, and especially about the part played by the Church of England in that movement.

The pages of history bear witness to the fact that schism breeds schism. Each group breaking off from Catholic unity has been the parent of further breaks — once the authority of the Mother-Church is rejected, the whole principle of authority is lost. The path back to unity is not a simple return of a prodigal ; nor is the reunion of Christendom something to be achieved by a magic formula whose main constituent is goodwill. The following pages will, in large measure, be but a list of obstacles to be overcome.

The present essay consists mainly of a study of the notion of the Church as found in contemporary Anglican theology. The writer believes — and in this he would be enthusiastically supported by many Anglicans — that it is only through a study of Anglican teaching about the Church that a true understanding of the Ecumenical Movement will be achieved, and one can truly say that if the Ecumenical Movement ever unites the non-Catholic churches, the resulting unity will be but a large-scale version of the Church of England.

It must always be of interest to the Catholic theologian to know what is being taught by those outside the church in order that he may be able to defend his own teaching and where necessary refute false doctrines. It must be confessed that Catholic theological treatises in general show a very poor knowledge of Anglican theology, and often what they know of it is gleaned at second-hand. They seem to know very little about Anglicanism beyond the fact that there are three parties in the Church of England and that Anglican Orders are invalid. Bishop Gore's kenotic teaching is sometimes mentioned, but very little else. Anglicans naturally believe that there is no answer to their position when they find it thus shunned by Catholic treatises. The publicity given of late to reunion questions has brought Anglican theology and especially Anglican doctrine on the church into the limelight, and in any future studies of the church, theologians cannot afford to ignore entirely the Anglican viewpoint.

In the following pages an attempt is made to present a general picture of Anglican thought with reference to reunion in the last sixty years. It would have been possible to follow the historical method, and to list each event, year by year, as it occurred. Such a method would undoubtedly produce a complete picture. It would, however, have many disadvantages. Hence I have approached the subject rather in a selective spirit, dealing with a few events at greater length, and saying little about other equally important problems if (to my way of thinking) they do not add much to our understanding of Anglican thought. Many readers would, I am sure, have preferred more reasoned comment on some of the conferences and reunion meetings mentioned, but I decided that, since the book is designed primarily for those not familiar with the Anglican scene, it would be better to let the accounts of these discussions speak for themselves, and I have added comments only whenever this appeared necessary.

A note on the Lambeth Conferences may be helpful here. These Conferences are gatherings of Archbishops and Bishops in communion with the See of Canterbury, (some being directly connected with it, others through their own Metropolitan or National Church), and meetings are held usually about every ten years for deliberation on questions of common interest to the bishops of the Anglican Communion. In the present essay we have used these reports and resolutions extensively without however burdening the text with the precise page-reference in each case, as this can be located without any difficulty in the reports themselves. It may, however, be helpful if a short explanation of the form of these reports is given.

Most of the reports contain an encyclical letter, the resolutions of the Conference and the reports of particular committees. We have referred throughout to committee reports as being the work of the Conference, though technically they possess only the authority of the committee which framed them. The following are the editions used in this essay :

For the Conferences from 1867 to 1908 inclusive :
The Six Lambeth Conferences, 1867-1920.

For the Conferences of 1920 and 1930 :
The Lambeth Conferences (1867-1930) .

For the Conferences of 1948 and 1958 :
the single volume reports *Lambeth Conference, 1948,* and *The Lambeth Conference, 1958,*

A further volume also frequently referred to is *Lambeth Occasional Reports 1931-8.* This contains reports of negotiations between Church of England representatives and other Churches between 1931 and 1938. A reference is usually given to the church involved in the negotiations thus : *Lambeth Occasional Reports* (Finland), p. 119.

The three volumes of reunion documents edited by Dr. G.K.A. Bell are of immense value to the student of Anglican theology, and they have already taken their place as a standard work of reference on the subject. The abbreviations commonly used in referring to them are as follows, and in the present essay this system is adhered to :

Documents on Christian Unity, 1920-1924 is called Bell, *Documents, I.*

Documents on Christian Unity, Second Series 1924-1930 is called Bell, *Documents, II.*

Documents on Christian Unity, Third Series 1930-1948 is called Bell, *Documents, III.*

All quotations from Papal Encyclicals on the question of reunion are taken from the edition by E. C. Messenger under the title *Rome and Reunion.*

CHAPTER I

THE CHURCH OF CHRIST IN ANGLICAN THEOLOGY

The idea is commonly found in Anglican theology that the Catholic Church possesses no clear statement on the doctrine of the church. St. Thomas, Anglicans point out, has no explicit treatment of the question in the *Summa Theologica,* and we are reminded that the Vatican Council defined only one of the twelve proposed canons on the subject. While this may be true, we must remember that there is a vast body of Catholic doctrine on the subject of the church which is beyond dispute, as will be shown by the fundamental sameness of all the standard Catholic treatises *de Ecclesia.* St. Thomas wrote at a time when the tract on the church was an integral part of Christology, and before the Reformation polemic gave it its present independent and apologetic form.

Catholic theologians, on the other hand, complain that Anglican theology refuses to make any clear and definite statement on the nature of Christ's Church. There is, they say, a refusal to define or, if a definition is given, an unwillingness to abide by the terms of the definition. Anglicans do not entirely reject this charge, and they admit that the reason why in the Church of England a pro-Roman party repeatedly arises is that the Church of England has no satisfying doctrine of the church. There is a constant appeal for a fuller realization on the part of Anglicans of what is actually meant by the church, and an admission that 'ever since the Reformation the Reformed Churches have been in a state of fumbling uncertainty . . . quite undecided what kind of Church they want, how it ought to be governed, what the conditions of membership should be, and where the seat of authority resides.'[1] Hence it is only natural that we should find it difficult to discover a satisfactory definition of the church in Anglican theology.

When we turn to the official and semi-official formularies of the Church of England, we note this difficulty immediately. There is some dispute or difficulty about every definition that is given. Thus Article XIX of the Thirty-nine Articles reads :

Ecclesia Christi visibilis est coetus fidelium, in quo verbum Dei purum praedicatur, et sacramenta, quoad ea quae necessario exigantur, juxta Christi institutum recte administrantur. Sicut erravit Ecclesia Hierosolymitana, Alexandrina, et Antiochena; ita et erravit Ecclesia Romana, non solum quoad agenda, et caeremoniarum ritus, verum in his etiam quae credenda sunt.	The visible Church of Christ is a congregation of faithful men, in which the pure Word of God is preached, and the Sacraments be duly administered according to Christ's ordinance in all those things that of necessity are requisite to the same. As the Church of Jerusalem, Alexandria, and Antioch have erred, so also the Church of Rome hath erred, not only in their living and manner of Ceremonies, but also in matters of Faith.

At first sight this would seem to be a definition of the visible universal church, but the history of the Article and the reference to local churches at the end suggest that it is rather a definition of a particular, local church.   The correct translation of the opening words would then be ' A visible church of Christ ', and the meaning would be particular, not universal.   The doctrine of the Church underlying the Article would appear to be an invisible, world-wide Church becoming visible in particular, local churches, the only tests of authenticity being the two notes mentioned. As has been frequently pointed out, the Article is an attempt at a wide definition which would include all the varieties of 'reformed' churches, while excluding the Catholic party.   However, very few Anglicans to-day would be willing to accept the two notes of the church which it proposes, namely, the preaching of the pure word of God and the right administration of the sacraments.   The Article is therefore unsatisfactory as a definition of the church.

This wide definition has some support in the resolutions of the various Lambeth Conferences.   The famous 'Appeal to all Christian People', issued by the 1920 Conference, acknowledges 'all those who believe in our Lord Jesus Christ, and have been baptized into the name of the Holy Trinity, as sharing with us membership in the universal Church of Christ which is His Body.' Elsewhere in the same Conference, we are told that the church is 'the whole society of Christian men.'

In 1946 there appeared the semi-official document *The Doctrine of the Church as held and taught in the Church of England*. It was written by a board of seven theologians, composed of the editor, three 'Catholics' and three Evangelicals. This booklet shows us the real cause of the difficulty of getting a suitable Anglican definition of the church — the opposing 'Catholic' and 'Protestant' tendencies in the Church of England. First we are given what we may call the 'Catholic' definition : 'Wherever in the formularies of the Church of England there is reference to the Church Universal, the reference is to whatever Christian bodies openly profess the faith of the oecumenical creeds and maintain the apostolic ministry by unbroken succession of ordinations.' Later we find an equally explicit 'Protestant' definition : 'In the mind of the Church of England the universal church is the society of men and women which Christ constituted as the fellowship of forgiven sinners to be the earthly body through which He should carry on His work in the world.' While this definition is not incorrect, its extreme vagueness makes it useless, and many Anglicans would not accept it without substantial qualifications. No effort is made to reconcile the two types of definition, or to show whether the 'Protestant' or the 'Catholic' one is the official teaching of the Church of England.

This dualism, if we may so call it, we shall meet frequently in Anglican theology, but it is here, perhaps, more than anywhere else, that it makes itself felt. When we come to the definitions given by individual theologians, we can immediately put them into one of two classes. We have first the strict Anglo-Catholic definition that the church is a visible society depending for its continued existence on episcopal organization derived from the apostles. The church would then include the Anglican, Roman, Old Catholic, Eastern Orthodox and perhaps the Scandinavian churches. All others would, theoretically at least, be outside. As against this view, Dr. Headlam puts forward as the official teaching of the Church of England that 'the Church does not consist only

of those of episcopal ministry but of all faithful people throughout the world, though they are unfortunately divided by
schism.'(²)   These two definitions cannot be reconciled with one
another.   Again, if we accept Bishop Gore's authority for defining the church as 'the extension and perpetuation of the incarnation in the world,' we shall be surprised to find a more modern
writer devoting a whole chapter to refuting that definition.(³)
To ask an Anglican theologian for a definition of the church is
to ask many more questions at the same time, and most Anglican
writers prefer to give a definition which carries no doctrinal
implications with it.

Since it is difficult to get a satisfactory definition of the church
from Anglican theologians, perhaps an examination of their teaching on the notes of the church will assist us.   Practically all
give the same four 'notes' as does Catholic theology, but these
notes are referred not to the church of Christ as it exists in fact
to-day.   A distinction is made between the ' actual ' and the
' ideal ' church, ' between the Church as it is in the world and the
Church as it is in God's idea.'(⁴)   The four notes, then, apply
in the full sense only to the ideal church ;   they are realized but
imperfectly in the church of to-day.   That unity for which
Christ prayed belongs to the ideal church ;   the actual church
has got it only imperfectly, and so it is divided by schism.
Christ's church is holy — ' a glorious church, not having spot or
wrinkle or any such thing '— but that holiness is said to belong
to the ideal church, and so we have sin in the church as it
is in the world.   So too with catholicity and apostolicity ;   the
church as it now exists is not fully catholic nor fully apostolic.
It is a church of the future, an ideal *in fieri,* requiring probably
tens of thousands of years to reach full actuality.(⁵)

We have already noted some definitions of the church which
make it clear that Anglicans do not restrict membership of the
church of Christ to members of their own communion.   The
question which we wish to examine here is :   Do Anglican
theologians place *any* limitation on membership of the church ?
Apart from some Anglo-Catholics, the common teaching seems
to be that any man who claims adherence to Christ is thereby a
member of Christ's church.   There is a definite unwillingness to
' unchurch ' anyone, whether it be the Society of Friends who

have no sacraments or the Unitarian who refuses to believe in the Blessed Trinity. In the early church, of course, the question of membership was a simple one, and those within the Christian society were entirely distinct from the Jewish and pagan worlds without. The Christians were then a distinct body, the *tertia gens*. To-day, however, the problem is not quite so simple, and various views are put forward by Anglican theologians.

The strange view was put forward in the last century by the great Anglican theologian F. D. Maurice that the church consists of the whole of mankind. Arguing from the fact that Christ is head of all men and head of the church as well, he refused to exclude from the church any single individual of the human race. We need not delay with this strange idea ; it it totally opposed to the teaching of the New Testament and Christian tradition, and it not defended by any theologian to-day.

The strict Anglo-Catholic view would, as we have seen, confine church membership to the episcopal communions. The Lambeth Appeal on the other hand admitted as full members 'all those who believe in our Lord Jesus Christ and have been baptized into the name of the Holy Trinity.' This statement of official Anglicanism is all the more important when we realize that it is contained in a document which may be said to be the real basis of the modern reunion movement, and perhaps the nearest thing to an Anglican declaration of faith that we have had for many years. Despite its quasi-official character, however, there is a decided tendency not to accept its full implications, and many Anglicans prefer to leave the question an open one. As was pointed out by Anglo-Catholic theologians, the Lambeth statement can be taken as declaring either that heretics and schismatics as organized bodies are part of the church, or that they belong to it as individuals in spite of their membership in these sects. In either case the statement is contrary to the consensus of patristic teaching.

The Congregational writer Cadoux tries to show that this wide notion of the membership of the church is taken from Congregationalist teaching, and proves his contention by a series of six arguments from the writings of Anglican theologians. This, he tells us, ' leads to the interesting conclusion that the rigid Anglo-Catholic definition of the Church has broken down, and that

many representative Anglicans are prepared to acknowledge —
implicitly or explicitly — the substantial truth of the inclusive
Congregational definition.' ([6]) Despite this claim, it would appear
that this wider view is taken not from Congregationalism, in
whose theology Anglicans have little interest, but from the
Modernist belief that the only test of church membership is the
confession that 'Jesus is Lord.' The Lambeth Appeal was framed
when Anglican modernism was at its height, and this attitude
to church membership is common in modernist writings of the
period.

If Anglican theology refuses to define in any strict sense its
terms of membership, it seems natural to ask : does Anglicanism
take seriously the doctrine that the church of Christ is a visible
society ? To this question Anglican theologians give the unan-
imous reply that the theory of an invisible church has no place
in their theology. It is, we are told, wholly unscriptural, and
at variance with scripture and the whole pre-Reformation teaching.
Bishop Gore claims that the idea has passed into disrepute, ([7])
and the Dutch theologian Visser t'Hooft informs us that it never
really took hold of Anglican theology. ([8]).

Despite these protestations, the more one reads of Anglican
theology, the more one is made aware of at least very strong
tendencies to the idea of an invisible church. There is the clear
distinction between the actual and the ideal church which we have
already noted; there is a refusal to predicate infallibility, and
indefectibility of the visible church, though it is generally admitted
that these belong to the church of Christ; and there is, finally,
the historical connection with Lutheranism which at least coloured
Anglican theology at its fountain-head.

The idea of a wholly invisible church, having already appeared
as an element of many earlier heresies, was resurrected by Luther
as a logical necessity, and became at once the central dogma of
most of the Continental systems. It is undeniable that many of
the English reformers fervently adhered to the Lutheran system,
and strove to impose it on the Church of England. Even if the
doctrine of the invisible church was not taught explicitly, the
premisses that led to it were clearly outlined, and the Anglican
mentality was conditioned against the whole idea of a universal
visible church.

Besides, it is important to note our earlier conclusion about the attitude of the Nineteenth Article. It defines 'ecclesia Christi visibilis' in Lutheran terminology, and we are not being unfair when we presuppose as its background the Lutheran idea of the universal church as invisible and becoming visible only in local, particular churches. Anglican theologians admit that the Article, 'read against the background of contemporary thought', ([9]) certainly does not exclude the idea of an invisible church, and there has never been an authoritative rejection of this interpretation by the Church of England. It is interesting to note that while Newman was an Anglican he could never make up his mind whether he believed in a visible or an invisible church.

We are left with the same general impression when we examine the teaching of Hooker, perhaps the greatest of Anglican apologists. While he often writes of the visible church as any Catholic theologian might write, he also clearly distinguished the visible from what he called the mystical church. ([10]) He was a Calvinist by education and upbringing, and Anglicans admit that he was a firm believer in the invisible church, if not to the end, at least in his earlier days.

The particular circumstances which made the theory of an invisible church popular in the sixteenth century are present to-day. The different sects at first firmly believed that they themselves exclusively constituted the church of Christ ; later, however, this exclusiveness ended, and the doctrine of the invisible church was called in as a suitable explanation of the various divisions. It solved the question of the unity of the church, and gave a *raison d'être* to the numerous sects which grew up as a result of the rejection to the visible unifying authority of the bishop of Rome.

The modern Reformed doctrine of the invisible church owes its origin mainly to Hatch and after him to Sohm, and in the present century Karl Barth has given it the central position in his theological system. This revival has had a marked influence on Anglican theology. The hostility between the various sects and denominations is gradually being broken down, mainly because of the reunion movement, and once a church denies that itself exclusively is the church of Christ, it must immediately take on the responsibility of finding a theology which will justify its remaining separated from Catholic unity. Protestant sects make full use of the invisible church in these circumstances, and the Church of England is finding it difficult to resist the temptation to follow them. Many of the schemes of reunion in which Anglicans are taking part, and which we shall examine later, are clearly based on a theory of an invisible church, and Anglican negotiators, intent on defending some of the less important elements of Anglican thought and practice, are apt to forget that they are sacrificing all by admitting that the church of Christ is primarily invisible. This is particularly obvious in the negotiations with the Free Churches, whose theology is mainly Lutheran.

We shall have to return often during the course of this essay to the position of Anglican theology in relation to the question of the invisible church. It will suffice to say here that if Anglicanism has never officially adopted the theory, neither has it officially rejected it. In this, as in many other problems, it insists on its duty of ' facing-both-ways ' and thus preparing the way for reunion by keeping in contact with the Catholic Church on the one hand and the Free Churches on the other.

Catholic teaching is uncompromising in regard to the unicity and unity of Christ's church. As there can be but one church, so this one church must be absolutely one. Not only is the church not divided, but it is indivisible. One in faith, sacraments, and apostolic government, it can never lose that unity which was given to it by its Divine Founder, and it points to the whole of the New Testament doctrine and whole history of the church in support of that teaching. The fourth gospel, itself a theology of unity, and the epistles of St. Paul, ' l'homme de l'unité '([11]) bear witness to the essential character of this unity, and scarcely a sect has been found that did not pay at least lip-service to unity as a note of the church.

The Anglican Church lays no claim to exclusiveness. It admits that there are bodies outside and independent of itself which are equally the church of Christ. Yet it professes to accept the New Testament teaching that the church is one. In what sense, we may ask, do the Church of England, the Eastern Orthodox, and other churches form one unit, and form it in such a way that all together merit the name of the one undivided Body of Christ ?

The number and variety of answers given to this question by Anglican theologians since the sixteenth century is very great. Refusing, as we have seen, to admit fully the theory of an invisible church, they were forced to take up the most difficult positions on the question of the church's unity, and had to use various metaphors to prove that, despite the undeniable disunity among the churches, real unity still existed. One simple means of avoiding the difficulty was, of course, to deny the disunity altogether, or at least to deny its reality, and not a few writers have taken up this position. For Bishop Gore, the common possession of the Holy Spirit is a guarantee that the disunion is only apparent and not real, while for other writers the same Creeds, Sacraments, ministry and supernatural life are links of unity beside which the differences appear merely as an 'interruption of Christian fellowship.'([12]). The Modernist teaching gets away from the difficulty by saying that the disunion is not only permissible but necessary for the well-being of the church : ' the Christ-Spirit has manifested Himself historically in divers forms and in divers manners ; the divisions of contemporary Christendom represent severally the various partial embodiments and aspects of His working.' ([13])

Apart from these few denials of the existence of any problem of unity, we find a common line of approach among Anglican theologians. There is first the admission that the visible unity of Christ's church is really broken — a fact which can scarcely be denied on Anglican principles — followed by a claim that there is a *spiritual, inward* or *fundamental* bond remaining, binding together the scattered fragments of Christ's church. This seems to be the view accepted by the Lambeth Conference of 1920 :

> The unity which we seek exists. It is in God, Who is the perfection of unity, the one Father, the one Lord, the one Spirit, Who gives life to the one Body. Again, the one Body exists. It needs not to be made, nor to be remade, but to become organic and visible. Once more, the fellowship of the members of the one Body exists. It is the work of God, not of man. We have only to discover it, and to set free its activities.

Analysing this statement, we can conclude from it : (i) that the unity sought has already real objective existence; (ii) that this unity is not now active or visible, and (iii) that it can be made visible by human activity.   Our problem, of course, mainly con-cerns the first of these three propositions : we are given no explanation of the nature of unity, nor are we told by what it is constituted.   The statement that the one Body needs ' to become organic and visible ' is strangely near the theory of an invisible church, and can scarcely have any meaning apart from that theory.

We are driven to conclude that this ' spiritual,' ' inward,' ' fund-amental ' unity is nothing but invisible unity under another name. The word ' invisible ' is never used in this context, but when we meet the term ' visible unity ' we always get the impression that it is being contrasted implicitly with its correlate, invisible unity, and that while visible unity belongs to particular churches, the church universal possesses only invisible unity.   There is, too, a fairly general refusal to discuss the church as the Body of Christ and to examine the implications of that metaphor.   One writer admits that ' the description of the Church as the Body of Christ is to be taken ontologically and realistically',(14) but he does not succeed in showing how the church as he conceives it can be said to be 'One Body'.   Apparently many Anglican theologians dislike the metaphor altogether, as if it were too difficult to explain in view of the present lack of visible unity among the non-Roman churches.   If we read the passages referred to above, and replace the words ' spiritual', ' inward', and ' fundamental', by the term ' invisible ' unity, the argument seems perfectly correct and logical. Anglicans would, however, shrink from drawing the obvious con-clusion that a church whose principle of unity is invisible is itself invisible, or as Dom Chapman comments on Bishop Gore's ideas of unity, it is ' a visible Church which needs have no visible unity'.(15) To put the point in another way :   in so far as the church of Christ is one, it is invisible.

One of the most striking contributions made by Anglicanism to the theology of the church is the theory of the Branch Churches as a solution of the problem of unity.   Though found in equivalent terms in the Caroline divines, it was not worked out fully until 1838 when William Palmer published his *Treatise on the Church of Christ.* At this period it was taken to cover only three communions, namely, the Anglican, Eastern Orthodox and Roman Churches, but to-day a ' branch ' is the equivalent of a ' portion ' or ' part' of the church, and can refer to any number of local or national churches, even outside of these three main communions.

It is difficult to know whether the branch theory of the church is to be taken as the official teaching of the Church of England. The terminology is certainly found on practically every page of Anglican writing on the church and has been canonized in many official documents. We shall quote only two examples taken more or less at random, one from the first and one from the 1948 Lambeth Conference. The report of the 1867 Conference was addressed ' to the faithful in Christ Jesus . . . in communion with the Anglican Branch of the Church Catholic', and the 1948 report defined the Anglican Communion as ' a portion of the Holy Catholic Church, independent of the Latin and Oriental branches of the Church.' Many examples could be quoted from the theologians, showing that at least the terminology, if not the doctrine, of the branch theory has been accepted. Explicit declarations that the theory itself is part of Anglican theology are by no means common, and Sheila Kaye-Smith is perhaps alone in claiming that it is essential to the Anglo-Catholic position.[16]

On the contrary, we find numerous rejections by Anglican theologians of both the terminology and doctrine of the branch theory. They realise, as Catholic theologians have repeatedly pointed out, that if the metaphor means anything, it means that the three or more branches belong to one trunk, and we are immediately face to face with the problem : where is that trunk now ? If the branches are living branches, as they must be, then they must exist in a living tree. There is also the further objection that if the trunk were in existence to-day, it could not possess three or more specifically different branches. Hence it is not surprising that one Anglican writer should admit that 'a more misleading metaphor it would be difficult to find,'[17] and another sums up the position well when he says that no verbal juggling can make three branches one.[18]

Of the other metaphors used by Anglican theologians to explain the unity of the church, we can give only the briefest outline. Perhaps the most popular is that of the family. The church we are told, is like a family, a single natural society, in which unfortunately the members are on bad terms with one another. Unity will come by common effort, by greater charity and especially by prayer.

A kindred idea is that which likens the unity of the church to that of a race or people who, while they may be divided as to outward organization, still remain a separate entity. The church is also likened to the sea, which is really one and undivided despite the fact that we give different names to different parts of it. Other metaphors would identify the church with a broken mirror or piece of china, with a parchment disfigured by rents but still readable, or more imaginatively still with a series of post-offices in which each local office has no independent rights but merely represents the General Post Office in one particular place.

Again, there seems to be a lack of realization among Anglicans that the unity of the church is from above, is a God-given thing. The whole reunion movement is based on the belief that man can at least restore the unity of the church, and it might be argued that if it is something which men can restore it is also something made by man in the first instance. This idea is totally at variance with the whole of Christian tradition, which sees in the unity of the church a projection, as it were, of that unity by which God Himself is eternally One.

The Anglican teaching on the nature of schism follows as a corollary from Anglican teaching on the nature of unity. It is pointed out that in the first Epistle to the Corinthians St. Paul is condemning a state of affairs which he calls by the name of schismata. Now it is generally admitted, and seems to be the more correct view, that these schismata were divisions *within* the body — that they were cliques or coteries within the church of Corinth rather than divisions which split its organic unity. Basing itself on this definition of schism as ' divisions within the body ', Anglican theology seeks to show that the various schisms which took place since the early centuries were all divisions within the one church, and did not break that ' spiritual,' ' inward ' and ' fundamental ' unity of which we have already spoken.

The argument is at first sight plausible enough. It means that if schism does not entail the breaking off of a part from a

whole which remains unaffected by the loss, then both parties are
in schism and not merely the part which 'breaks off.' Thus the
1938 Report on Church of England doctrine tells us : ' It should
be recognised that " schism " is, in fact, a division within the
Christian Body. That Body is not to be thought of as consisting
of a single true Church or group of Churches, with a number of
" schismatic " bodies gathered about it, but as a whole which is
in a state of division or "schism".'([19]) This is the almost universal
teaching of Anglican theologians. There is, we are told, no real
difference in kind between a quarrel of two Christian neighbours
and a schism between two churches. Both are examples of want
of charity within the church.

   This suggested solution is unfortunately an over-simplification.
We readily admit that for St. Paul ' schismata ' meant something
different from what we usually mean when we use the word to-day.
We deny, however, the identification of the facts covered by the
two different usages of the term — we deny, that is, that the
situation to-day corresponds with the divisions in the church of
Corinth in St. Paul's day. To-day the divisions among the various
churches are as wide and as fundamental as they could possibly be.
Even the central dogmas of Christianity are in dispute between the
different denominations, unlike the Christian church where the
whole depositum of apostolic teaching was faithfully received,
and where disputes were confined to personal loyalties and details
of hero-worship. There is no adequate parallel between the situation envisaged in the first epistle to the Corinthians and the
situation among the non-Roman churches to-day. Catholic
theology rightly defines schism as ' rebellion against the authority
of legitimate ecclesiastical superiors.' Schism is the wilful cutting
oneself off from the unity of the body, and this body, though
possibly losing much by the separation, retains its unity unimpaired.

   Side by side with the affirmation that all churches are in schism
goes the affirmation that many of the heresies of the early church
were not really heresies at all, or at least that the divisions which
resulted from them were caused mainly by the intransigence of
the central body in refusing to accept reasonable interpretations
of doctrine. There is also the belief that the descendants of these
early heretics no longer hold the particular tenets for which their
forefathers left the church, and a general readiness to assume

their orthodoxy. The Lambeth Conferences have been especially liberal in this respect. We may question the possibility of a change of doctrine in these sects, and may well ask : Is it not rather that the Anglican concept of heresy has tended to disappear of late years ? Schism and heresy are two traditional concepts in Catholic theology which have been emptied of all their content by modern Anglican thought.

In the foregoing pages we have examined briefly some of the more general aspects of Anglican theology on the nature of the church of Christ. While as Catholics we disagree with much of it, we must nevertheless point out that there is a fundamental consistency in the Anglican approach to all of these questions. The teaching on membership agrees with the teaching on unity, and the teaching on schism follows from both. If Anglican ecclesiology is in part incorrect, incoherent it certainly is not.

This fundamental coherence of teaching is one of attitude rather than of principle. Its basis is that of general toleration and broadmindedness in theology which are part of the Anglican ethos. This ethos we must try to understand more closely by an examination of the Church of England under that aspect in which it frequently presents itself — the Church of England, National and Comprehensive.

NOTES TO CHAPTER I

(1) W. R. Inge, *The Church and the Age*, p. 57.

(2) *Lambeth Occasional Reports*, (Latvia and Estonia), p. 234.

(3) J. E. L. Newbigin, *The Reunion of the Church*, p. 55 ff. The title of Chapter V. is ; 'The Extension of the Incarnation ?' Strictly speaking, Newbigin is not an Anglican but a member of the new Church of South India.

(4) Alfred Blunt, *What the Church Teaches*, p. 61.

(5) Inge, op. cit., p. 67. For an Anglican refutation of this distinction between the 'actual' and the 'ideal' church, see W. Lock in Gore, *Lux Mundi*, p. 274.

(6) C. J. Cadoux, in Mackenzie, *Union of Christendom*, ii. 513.

(7) Charles Gore, *The Holy Spirit and the Church*, p. 52.

(8) W. A. Visser t'Hooft, *Anglo-Catholicism and Orthodoxy*, p. 17.

(9) L. Hodgson (Ed.), *The Doctrine of the Church as held and taught in the Church of England*, p. 17.

(10) Cf. the passage quoted in More and Cross, *Anglicanism*, p. 41. See also G. K. A. Bell, *Christian Unity*, p. 12 ff.

(11) L. Cerfaux, *L'Église des Corinthiens*, p. 104. For St. Paul's teaching on the unity of the church, see the same writer's *La Théologie de l'église suivant saint Paul*, p. 175 ff.

(12) H. B. Swete, *The Holy Catholic Church*, p. 14.

(13) A. E. J. Rawlinson, in *Foundations*, p. 403. See also H. Rashdall, *Christus in Ecclesia*, p. 324, for the same idea.

(14) E. L. Mascall, *Christ, the Christian, and the Church*, p. 112.

(15) Dom J. Chapman, *Bishop Gore and the Catholic Claims*, p. 21.

(16) Sheila Kaye-Smith, *Anglo-Catholicism*, p. 169. This work was, of course, written before the writer's conversion to the Catholic Church.

(17) H. L. Gouge, *The Church of England and Reunion*, p. 326.

(18) A. C. Headlam, *The Doctrine of the Church and Christian Reunion*, p. 215.

(19) *Doctrine in the Church of England*, p. 112.

CHAPTER II

THE CHURCH OF ENGLAND, NATIONAL AND COMPREHENSIVE

In the last analysis, what the Church of England believes about the nature of the church of Christ will be based on what it believes about itself. If it believes itself to be a part of an undivided and indivisible whole, under the authority of a visible head, it must as a consequence hold very definite views about the nature of the universal church. But if on the other hand it believes that it is the church of the English nation, independent of other churches and allowing no allegiance to any higher organisation, then its theology on the subject of the universal church must be conditioned by these beliefs.

The Church of England has never claimed to be exclusive. It has never claimed more than that it is a part of the church of Christ, or as some writers prefer to put it, it is the church of Christ in England. The exclusive claims of Rome and the Eastern Orthodox Churches are looked upon with complete scepticism and pointed out as proof that these communions are out of touch with reality. The Church of England is therefore nearer to reality when she claims that she is only 'part of the One Holy Catholic and Apostolic Church,' and a ' true and undoubted part of this divinely created organism.'([1]) 'Anglicans do not claim,' says another writer, ' to have a church of their own, but to be an integral part of the one Catholic Church of Christ . . . that part of the Catholic Church which is established in this country.'([2]) The same principles apply to the Anglican Communion—though existing in practically every country in the world, it lays no claim to be the whole church. The opening clauses of the Lambeth Encyclicals are interesting in this respect, as the bishops style themselves as follows : ' We, Archbishops and Bishops of the Holy Catholic Church in full communion with the Church of

16

England.' The claim put forward is that they are bishops of the Holy Catholic Church, not that they alone constitute the whole Catholic episcopate. ' There are other families of Churches in the Church Universal.' When a Russian bishop asked for consec-ration as a bishop of the Anglican Communion, Archbishop Davidson told him : ' Your Lordship is under a misconception as to the position and function of the English Church. We make no claim to a universal mission.'(³). The Church of England, then, does not believe that it is more than the church of the English nation ; it is content to be a national church.

The theory of autonomous national churches may seem to us Catholics to be contrary to the whole idea of the church as presented in the New Testament and in early Christian tradition, but it is now one of the central dogmas of Anglican theology and is defended with a wealth of proof both from scripture and tradition. The 1930 Lambeth Conference gives it as a basis for its definition of the churches of the Anglican Communion : ' They are " particular or national " Churches, and they repudiate any idea of a central authority.' Elsewhere the report distinguishes two types of church government : the first is that centralized form which is found in the Church of Rome, while the second is ' that of regional autonomy within one fellowship.' Dr. Headlam, speak-ing at the Lausanne Conference in 1927 stated clearly the Anglican position when he said : ' For me, the building up of one national Church in any nation in close union with the state seems the ideal to be attained.'(⁴)

This teaching is fully accepted by the High Church party. In May, 1922 a declaration of Anglican faith was sent to the Pat-riarch and Synod of Constantinople in an effort to influence that church to declare in favour of the validity of Anglican orders. Part of the declaration reads : ' We affirm that each particular Church is rightly independent (autokephalos) and self-administered (autodioketos)' in matters which are not essential to the faith or practice of the Universal Church.'(⁵) Granted that the declaration was drawn up with a definite purpose in view, and granted that in many other respects it is openly at variance with official Anglican teaching, it nevertheless expresses fairly well the Anglican doctrine on this subject. It is generally taken for granted, too, as this declaration takes for granted, that the Eastern churches are, like the Church of England, national autonomous bodies. It is more correct, however, to visualize them as local groupings built around the ancient patriarchates, to which a number of further patriarchates have added themselves in the course of time.

If we look for the origin of the idea of national churches, independent of one another and of any central authority, we shall really be looking for the origin of nationality itself. We are told that already in the eleventh century the Western Church was showing signs of developing into a number of independent churches, helped especially by the then common formula of a king as 'Rex-Sacerdos.' The power of kings and emperors over the appointment of bishops gave a strong impression that the church in each territory was merely an instrument for the development of the nation. Thus the theory grew until the sixteenth century when the rejection of papal authority left the field open for the full acceptance of the doctrine of an invisible church becoming visible in national churches.

Many Anglican theologians, in an effort to show that the reformation in England was merely the culmination of a long process of rejection of papal supremacy, have tried to show that from the earliest times the Ecclesia Anglicana had shown a particularly independent and nationalistic spirit. They point to the implications of the very name 'Ecclesia Anglicana,' and its parallel with the title 'Ecclesia Gallicana' which had a very definite nationalistic meaning even in the middle ages. The constant protests against the giving of English benefices to Italians, the statutes of Provisors and Praemunire, and the famous 'Ecclesia Anglicana libera sit' of the Magna Charta are all brought forward in support of this argument. The conclusion is that when Henry VIII rejected papal supremacy and declared himself head of the church he was acting merely as the organ and mouth-piece of four hundred years of English nationalism.

Convincing as this argument may seem, it is rejected even by many Anglican scholars. Thus Z. N. Brooke admits that he began his study with the general impression that in the early years the English church was already showing a very independent spirit, but he admits : 'what I have discovered has changed my point of view completely. As I now see it, the English Church was in mind at one with the Church as a whole throughout the period.'(6)

He shows conclusively that the phrase Ecclesia Anglicana had no narrow nationalistic meaning in this early period, and points out that the declaration ' Ecclesia Anglicana libera sit ' has a meaning which should be obvious to anyone who reads the Magna Charta— it is a declaration of the freedom of the Church of England not from papal supremacy but from the interference of a national-minded king, and as such it received the blessing of Pope Innocent III.   It is further admitted that papal supremacy, at least in matters spiritual, was fully accepted in pre-reformation England, and that the Pope was also recognized as the fountain-head of ecclesiastical law.   The various statutes of Provisors were enacted not primarily to exclude the possibility of papal nominations to English sees, but to guarantee that these sees would be available for bestowal on clerics in the civil service in place of monetary remuneration.   England was at one with the rest of Christendom in accepting the provisions of Roman Canon Law.

Nevertheless we are forced to admit that English nationalism played a big part in leading up to the break with Rome.   All the authors whom we have quoted as holding that England fully accepted the papal claims, agree that at the beginning of the six-teenth century nationalism was a force to be reckoned with in the Church of England.   The principle of nationalism was all the time gaining ground, and the final acceptance of the reform-ation by the English church must be traced ultimately to the acceptance of that principle.

It is clear today that Henry VIII had no idea of founding a new church — he merely wanted to reject the Pope's inter-vention in what he considered to be the private affairs of the Church of England.   In this connection Henry's *Assertio Septem Sacramentorum* is particularly interesting :   Luther's identification of Rome with the scarlet woman of Babylon (Apoc. xvii) is vividly repudiated :

> ' What serpent ever crawled so poisonously as this man who gives the name of Babylon to the Holy Roman See, calls the Supreme Pontiff its evil mistress, thinks that his salutary decrees mean slavery for the whole Church, and makes the name of the most holy Pontiff into antichrist !   What a limb of the devil is he, who seeks to tear away Christians, the members of Christ, from their head ! '(7)

If it be admitted that this kind of writing is in any way typical of the first English reactions to Luther, it shows that despite the strength of nationalism in England the papal claims were accepted in all their fulness. It is very much open to discussion what might have happened if Henry had not made up his mind to divorce Catherine of Aragon. What is certain is that, given the opportunity, English nationalism was the main force which within the short space of a few years succeeded in detaching England from the papacy and in making of the Ecclesia Anglicana something it was not before — an autonomous national church whose Supreme Head was the king of England : ' the King our Sovereign Lord, his heirs and successors, Kings of this realm, shall be taken, accepted and reputed the only Supreme Head in earth of the Church of England called *Ecclesia Anglicana.*'

Anglican theologians generally appreciate the tremendous power exerted by nationalism in the sixteenth-century break. A lot depends, of course, on the individual writer's attitude to the reformation, but most of them agree that, at least in its early phase, the English reformation was little more than ' an extreme assertion of nationalism,'[8] and the modern hatred of the papacy can be traced to the feeling that the ' foreign priest ' was obstructing the rise of a great nation.[9]

Once the schism was completed, Henry had to provide a theological justification for it. As early as 1537 we find this justification fully worked out. The work known as the ' Bishops' Book,' published in that year, is the first explicit definition in Anglican theology of the church of Christ as a loose federation of national churches, none of which has any superiority over the others. Because of the close similarity of this theory to the teaching of William of Occam and Marsilius of Padua, it is at least *a priori* likely that it was taken from these writers by the theologians of Henry's reign. The real identity of the two streams of thought was brought out clearly in the opening years of the eighteenth century, when the Archbishop of Canterbury, William Wake, began a noted correspondence on the subject of reunion with the Gallican theologian Dupin. Although nothing eventually came of the matter, it showed clearly that the Ecclesia Anglicana and the Ecclesia Gallicana had very much the same teaching on the subject of the national church.

In the eyes of many Anglican theologians, the papacy both in the sixteenth century and to-day stands forth as the great enemy of nationalism. They seem to forget that the Catholic Church fully endorses and blesses the principle of nationalism, and that she accepts the fact that in the Old Testament God chose a nation and made His salvation available to the wold only through the channel of this chosen people. The Catholic Church teaches, too, that each nation must express Christianity through its own national forms, and she commands her missionaries not to impose their own nationality on those whom they are evangelizing ; they must rather help them to accept what is vital and essential in Christianity without making them less faithful to their own nation as a result. With the principle of nationality itself the church has no quarrel.

The sphere of nationality in the Christian faith is, however, limited by the very nature of that Christian faith itself. One Anglican writer expresses this limitation well :

> Nationality must not touch the deposit of the Faith. This it can neither increase nor diminish. It is concerned mainly with modes and methods of presentation of the one Truth. It must only present the one Faith, but that Faith may be tinged, coloured, hallowed by the equally God-given principle of nationality. [10]

Rightly interpreted, that statement is acceptable, but we contend that what the author condemns is precisely what has been done and is being done by national churches, namely, tampering with the essentials of the Christian faith. We hope to show later that in England at least a national church involves the notion of a comprehensive church — a church in which it matters only in a very secondary way what one believes. That is our fundamental objection to the theory of the national church : there can be no ' nationalizing ' of the fundamental doctrines of the Christian revelation.

Many Anglican writers are beginning to realize that nationalism is, like private judgment, something which can be over-emphasised, and they are beginning to see that the Church of England has very definitely over-emphasised it. This was a favourite theme with Bishop Gore, who pointed out that attaching too much importance to the national aspect of the church completely did away with the

New Testament notion of a supra-national universal church. ' We have been so content to be a national Church,' he writes, ' that we have forgotten our vocation to proclaim a supernational, universal, catholic fellowship.' Archbishop Davidson, speaking of Gore's attitude to nationalism and his own says : ' Bishop Gore of Oxford regards me as perilously lax in what I teach and practise as regards the National character of the Church of England, a phrase to which he has a special antipathy'.([11])

It is being generally realized, too, that ultra-nationalist ideas will eventually ruin the whole reunion movement, unless something is done to curb the present influence of nationalism on religion. If the reunion movement becomes merely a grouping of autonomous national churches, then it must be prepared to see those churches more interested in principles of nationalism than in principles of religion. Thus one writer confesses : ' It must be obvious from the beginning that the national spirit is going to be the chief difficulty in realizing the ideal of a Catholic Church.'([12]) In the mission-field the principle of nationalism is producing such anomalies as the new Church of South India, which we shall discuss later, and negotiations are going on all over the world for national churches on this model. It is obvious that the next two or three Lambeth Conferences are going to have many serious difficulties because of these new national churches.

Symptomatic, perhaps, of this realization of the dangers of nationalism is the readiness to concede that the terms 'national' and 'Anglican ' church are now out of date and should be replaced by something more expressive of the actual state of things. Thus T. S. Eliot admits that ' the word *national* in this context can no longer mean what it once meant,'([13]) and the 1948 Lambeth Conference expressed dissatisfaction at the use of the name 'Anglican ' for that group of churches which follows the Anglican ideal of the church. There is a definite tendency in Anglican theology to-day to speak more and more of the ' Catholic ' Church, and it is obvious that the authorities of the Church of England would be only too willing to assume the title ' the Catholic Church ' but for the fact that it would clash with the Anglican repudiation of exclusiveness and would deny the claim of the Anglican Communion to be a part, but only a part, of the Catholic Church.

Still it is not unlikely that a new name will be found for the Anglican Communion in the near future.

There is nowadays very little mention of one particular application of the principle of nationalism which was common in earlier Anglican theologians. Taken to its logical conclusion, the principle of nationalism would imply that there can be but one church for each nation : to be outside the national church is to be guilty of the sin of schism. It would imply further that an Englishman should attend Anglican worship in England, but if he crossed to France he should attend a Catholic church (seeing that the Catholic Church is admitted to be the national church of France), and in Germany a Lutheran church.

A little consideration should have shown the impossibility of such a theory being translated into practice. It takes no account of those countries in which there is no national church, or in which rival bodies are claiming that title, and it brands with schism the Church of Ireland and many other Churches of the Anglican Communion which cannot in any real sense be said to be the Church of the nation. It would also reject the claims of the Free Churches, and that is something which Anglican theologians are unwilling to do, at least explicitly, while there is still a hope that the Free Churches may come back and reunite with the Church of England. The Church of England cannot afford to forget that fundamentally the Anglican and Free Church apologetic are identical, for both are based on the principle that schism from the parent body can in certain circumstances be lawful.

Nationalism, then, is a dangerous principle when taken too far in religious matters. The Catholic Church has rightly kept a careful watch on all nationalist movements. She has blessed what was good in them, but she has been very severe on what was incompatible with the truths of faith, and Anglicans admit that this policy has been fruitful in results. ' It is an undoubted strength of the Roman Church that it does in a measure transcend these barriers,' writes Clarke, and his conclusion is that 'nationalism is not, and never can be, a fundamental principle on which the Church can be built.'([14]) The warning issued by the 1930 Lambeth Conference sounds like a confession, for it tells us that a national church ' must be on its guard lest the spirit of nationalism weaken its loyalty to the whole Catholic Church, lest it lend itself to unworthy political ends, and lest it expose itself to undue interference by the secular state'. To Catholic readers this passage must necessarily appear as an epitome of the history of the Church of England since the sixteenth century.

The theory of a national church implies that all who belong to the nation should belong to the national church as well. History, however, has shown would-be reformers that a nation is not as homogeneous a unit as they would wish it to be, and in every national church there have been groups unwilling to accept the doctrine or doctrines put forward by the central authority. Two methods have been tried in dealing with such dissenters. The first way, coercion, has been found to be a failure in practically every case. The alternative is to make room for the dissenters in matters of doctrine — that is, to widen the formularies of faith so as to make them acceptable, and thus the national church becomes a 'comprehensive' church.

That the Church of England is comprehensive to-day is the proud boast of many Anglicans. Whatever view we may take of its origin, the existence of three central parties, each holding radically different views of the Christian faith, and yet continuing to live together in a single national church, makes 'comprehensiveness' one of the most interesting and most striking characteristics of modern Anglicanism. The High Church party, ranging from 'ultra-Roman' Anglo-Catholics to men who accept the name of Catholic and little more, stands generally for a 'Catholic' interpretation of the Christian revelation, and would look forward ultimately to union with the see of Rome. The Evangelical or Low Church party, on the other hand, is the lineal descendant of the Lutheran reformers in the Church of England in the sixteenth century, and its members abhor everything that might in any way appear to be derived from Rome. The third or Modernist group, replacing the old Broad Church party, to a certain degree penetrates both Catholic and Evangelical parties, and stands for more or less the same principles as the modernist movement in the Catholic Church at the beginning of the present century. The parties do not, of course, possess clearly-defined limits, and the result is 'a spectrum which extends from right wing Catholicism to fundamentalist Protestantism, and of which the colours shade imperceptibly into each other.'([15])   The effect of this upon doctrine is obvious to anyone reading the literature emanating from the writers of the different groups. The three parties are often more hostile to one another than they are to non-Anglicans, and the constant friction is ever threatening to rend asunder the Church of England. We can well understand what Archbishop Lang meant when he said of his predecessor Davidson that he 'handled the three horses, Evangelical, Modernist, and Catholic, fairly and adroitly, but he always seemed to me more concerned to get them round the next corner than to envisage what the ultimate course of the journey was to be.'([16])

Great as has been the influence of parties within the Church of England on comprehensiveness of doctrine, far greater has been that exercised by the growth of the Anglican Communion and by the contacts of the Church of England with other churches abroad.

These young national churches, finding themselves received on equal footing with the parent church, are unwilling to reject doctrines which appeal to them, merely on the ground that they are not held in the Church of England. The result is that these opinions become tolerated in the whole Anglican Communion, and Anglicanism becomes more and more comprehensive. The great contemporary movement for reunion is also a great incentive to tolerance of other Churches' doctrine, or at least to refusal to condemn it as contrary to the Christian revelation.

The doctrine of comprehension is justified theologically on the ground that by means of it the church possesses 'all truth'. Christianity, we are told, is so vast a system of truth that no man can hope to possess more than part of it, and therefore it is necessary that different men and different parties should add up the little each possesses in order that the church may possess all truth. 'It may even be necessary to the Church,' says the Lambeth Encyclical of 1930, 'that men in it should hold and expound different opinions, in order that the Church as a whole should have the whole of truth.'

With this interpretation of the meaning of the words 'all truth' we can have little sympathy. If theology consists of definite beliefs about the nature of God and the nature of God's relations with man, then real knowledge of God will never be attained by the mere juxtaposition of a number of contradictory statements on these subjects. To say that our knowledge of God and man can never rise above such a congeries of conflicting opinions is to condemn the human mind to indifferentism and ultimately to agnosticism.

Many Anglican theologians could be quoted as paying homage to the doctrine of comprehension. ' To-day,' writes Dr. Wand, ' with the new movement totwards reunion, we have begun to discover again that comprehension is a noble, even a divine principle'. ([17]) For the modernist, of course, comprehensiveness is simply another name for his own theory of the nature of religious truth, and so we find Rashdall stating that of all the reasons which justify the retention of the Establishment, the most powerful is that it tends to cause comprehensiveness and liberalism in theo-logy.([18]) The 1948 Lambeth Conference fully endorsed the principle of comprehension by the sweeping admission that

> ' it is only through a comprehensiveness which makes it possible to hold together in the Anglican Communion under-standings of truth which are held in separation in other churches, that the Anglican Communion is able to reach out in different directions, and so to fulfil its special vocation as one of God's instruments for the restoration of the visible unity of His whole Church.'

We have given this passage in full because it is a good example of the Anglican habit of making a virtue of necessity. If the Church of England cannot get rid of comprehension, then com-prehension must be shown to be something worth while, something which the Church of England alone is fortunate enough to possess. From being a liability, it is made out to be a gift of God, and of special value to the reunion of the church.

Comprehensiveness seems such a good English virtue to-day that Anglicans make an effort to read it back into the first formularies of their church. We are thus presented with a picture of Anglicanism as a comprehensive church from the very beginning, and particular insistence is laid on the claim that the Thirty-nine Articles are, and were meant to be, comprehensive. The aim of the Articles was, we are told, to embrace as many as possible and to reduce the number of likely recusants. This case is strengthened by a whole series of works in which a Catholic meaning is taken from the Articles, and it appears conclusive when we see the Anglo-Catholic party claiming that it finds nothing in the Articles that cannot be squared with the doctrine of the church of Rome. Newman in Tract 90 claimed that ' the interpretation they (Anglo-Catholics) take was intended to be admissible ; though not that which their authors took themselves.'([19])

To claim that the Thirty-nine Articles were so framed as to include as many people as possible is to reject all the evidence. The wording of the Articles in nowhere abiguous ; they are plain statements of doctrine framed by a Protestant party which had no wish to keep the Catholic party within the national church. Dr. Messenger's conclusion to a close and scholarly study is that the Articles are 'uncompromisingly Protestant'.([20]) Up to Newman's time the only interpretation admitted was the Protestant one, and the storm that broke after Tract 90 showed up Newman as an innovator. Anyone who reads the Tract will realize that from the beginning Newman was arguing the impossible. The Anglican theologians at the Malines Conversations doubted the possibility of reconciling the Articles with Catholic doctrine, and Newman himself admitted that they are the ' offspring of an uncatholic age.' Hooft is correct when he says that Tract 90 was ' a strong expression of Newman's tendency to project his own convictions back into the life of the Church.'([21]) The Catholic interpretations which he puts on some of the Articles amount to a simple denial of the plain and unambiguous meaning of the words, and those Anglo-Catholics to-day who follow Newman in trying to show that the Articles are compatible with the decrees of Trent have to adopt the same evasive attitude. So far are the Articles from being ambiguous and comprehensive that they formally contradict some of the doctrines which had a short time previously been defined at Trent.

As we have already noted, comprehensiveness is one of the proudest possessions of Anglicans. And yet, as in the case of nationalism, we find not a few writers who condemn the principle outright, or at least admit that it can be taken to extremes. Vidler quotes F. D. Maurice as saying that while compromise can be at its best a virtue, it can, if taken too far, become a blight,([22]) and Bishop Gore, summing up his own attitude to comprehension as compared with that of Archbishop Davidson, said that he had always desired that the Church of England should be 'the home of a wide toleration ; but a toleration which had declared limits.'([23])

A still more striking repudiation of comprehensiveness is that put forward by the High Church writer, A. G. Hebert. He believes that it is quite a novel element in Anglican theology, and points out that ' no such motive (as comprehension) prevented the ejection of the Nonconformists in 1662, or the secession of the Nonjurors in 1689, or the persecution of the Tractarians, or the prosecution of the Ritualists'. The theory, he believes, appeared only at the end of the nineteenth century, and then only under the influence of theological liberalism, and he looks on it as one of the great evils of modern Anglican thought. The only way to reunion, he concludes, is that of ' unity in the truth,' and he condemns comprehensiveness as 'a weakening of grasp on the primacy of truth.'([24])   With this conclusion Catholic theology is in complete agreement.

The theory of comprehensiveness has completely done away with the true notion of dogma in the Church of England. Faith as an assent of the mind to definite revealed truths has almost disappear-ed. ' In regard to faith,' Dr. Goudge tells us quite unashamedly, ' nothing is *de fide* in the Church of England except the Creeds, and there are legitimate differences about their interpretation.'([25]) This statement, though it would be vigorously denied by many Anglo-Catholics, gives a factual picture of the situation, and we are inclined to agree with Jenkins when he says that from one point of view the Church of England can hardly be called a church at all — it is merely the *settlement* of the 'religious question' in England.([26])   And when the bishops assembled at the Lambeth Conference speak of 'our unity in the faith of Christ,' we wonder whether they are speaking of that ' fides fiducialis' dear to the Lutheran reformers or the ' religious attitude' acclaimed by the modernists. At least it is not faith in the traditional Catholic sense.

Of the position of the Church of England as the *Via Media* much has been written since Newman's time. We are interested in the idea here only in so far as it is related to the idea of comprehensiveness which we have been examining, and to the theory of the ' Bridge-Church ' to which the via media seems to be yielding place. In its simplest form, the via media means that the Church of England possesses a certain body of religious truth, purely Catholic and faithful to the scriptures, some of which Protestantism has wrongly rejected and to which Rome has added novel doctrines. Though T. S. Eliot would have us believe that the via media is Elizabethan in origin, it is clear that it is a Tractarian idea, developed with a conscious eye on the principle ' virtus in medio stat,' and as a theological justification for the existence of the Church of England.

The theory of the via media was never a successful one. Newman admitted that it never existed except on paper, and a modern exponent of the idea tells us that its genius ' lies in an obstinate adherence to principles which are apparently inconsistent with one another, which it holds in a working synthesis without pushing any one of them to its logical conclusion, or attempting to define their respective powers with precision.' (27) That was the strength, as well as the weakness, of the via media : it refused to see difficulties where difficulties really existed. It was an effort to find a middle way where no middle way existed, and its failure was a confession that Catholicism and Protestantism do not mix.

Since the via media has been recognized to be insufficient, another theory must be found to take its place, and the new theory which most Anglicans put forward is that of the Bridge-Church. It differs from the via media in one very important respect, namely, that the via media claimed to be really a mean between two sets of opposing doctrines, while the Bridge-Church claims, under the influence of the theory of comprehensiveness, to include both. Less difficult to defend than the via media, and in full agreement with contemporary thought on comprehensiveness, the Bridge-Church idea has been enthusiastically sponsored by Anglican writers as the most important factor in the reunion movement. It is thus outlined by the 1930 Lambeth Conference :

> Our special character and, as we believe, our peculiar con-
> tribution to the Universal Church, arises from the fact that,
> owing to historic circumstances, we have been enabled to
> combine in our fellowship the traditional Faith and Order of
> the Catholic Church with that immediacy of approach to
> God through Christ to which the Evangelical Churches es-
> pecially bear witness, and freedom of intellectual enquiry.

While the Bridge-Church theory is not mentioned explicitly here it is obviously the idea underlying the passage, and it is implied in the Anglican claim that the Church of England is the nucleus around which the future church is to be built.

Granted Anglican principles, the idea is an entirely logical development of the theory of comprehension. The Church of England to-day is admittedly the ' locus of dialectic between different interpretations of God's revealed will for His Church.'(28) Within the unity of the Established Church there exist divisions and differences which are almost exact replicas of the divisions among the churches seeking reunion. It is, so the argument runs, obviously God's will that the Church of England should keep up contact with the opposing Christian churches — the Catholic end of the bridge keeping ever in touch with the Roman Communion, and the Evangelical section maintaining friendly relations with the Free Churches. In this way, we are told, reunion will one day be brought about. At Malines it was stated that Anglicans generally believed that their own church had been placed by God in an intermediate position which involved responsibilities towards other churches, and it was implied that, in any steps taken towards reunion with Rome, the Eastern Orthodox and the Nonconformists could not be forgotten.(29)

In this theory we cannot fail to see at least a glimpse of national pride. The Church of England, for so long an isolated national Church, is glad at last to be able to show itself as the centre around which the great future church is to be built. Everywhere we meet with reflections of self-congratulation and a willingness to show how perfect an instrument is the Church of England for the unification of the scattered fragments of Christ's church. We meet this frequently in the reunion schemes, and particularly in some phases of the Ecumenical Movement. Of the position of the Church of England as a bridge, T. S. Eliot writes in typical Anglican fashion : ' In such difficult negotiations the Church is quite properly and conscientiously facing-both-ways : which only goes to show that the Church of England is at the present juncture the one church upon which the duty of working towards reunion most devolves.' The writer does not seem at all troubled by the risk of feeling, as he says, ' more orthodox when transacting with the Eastern and Baltic Churches, and more Evan-gelical when transacting with the Nonconformists.'([30]) We might add, ' the risk of feeling more Catholic when treating with the Romans.'

The idea of the Bridge-Church stands or falls with the doctrine of comprehensiveness. If comprehensiveness is a providential note of the Church of England, then that church is meant to be the bridge at which the opposing forces of Catholicism and Protestant-ism will one day come to terms. If on the other hand we believe that comprehensiveness is but another name for religious indiffer-entism, we must immediately condemn the principle of 'facing-both-ways ' and point out that the Church of England must become either Catholic or Protestant, since it cannot logically be both. As Fr. Walker declares, if the Church of England claims to be Catholic, it should press forward to re-union with the Catholic Church and cut adrift entirely from Protestantism; or if it wants to be fully a Reformation church it should unite with the Lutherans and Nonconformists.([31]) By trying to face both ways and to please both sides it has succeeded in pleasing neither, and the Archbishop of York was forced to admit that ' the situation of this " bridge " is so dangerous, that we must sometimes close it at both ends in order to make sure that it should not collapse in the middle.'([32]) The Catholic Church emphatically rejects the claim of the Church of England to be a Bridge-Church. The Free Churches are equally emphatic in rejecting it, and give many reasons for their attitude. The Eastern Orthodox deny the need of a ' bridge ' at all, since according to their theology the Ortho-dox alone constitute the true church, and both Catholicism and Protestantism must become Orthodox before reunion can become a reality.

It is difficult to foresee what will be the ultimate result of the interaction of the three notions which we have been examining in the present chapter, namely nationalism, comprehension and the Bridge-Church idea. As we have tried to show, the three are very closely connected, and they are undoubtedly the three out-standing characteristics of the Church of England to-day. Despite the objections which we have quoted from Anglican writers against the first two, there is no likelihood of these notions being

repudiated.   They are as near as we can get to the essence of
Anglican theology on the church.

It might seem that after examining the Bridge-Church idea we
might go on immediately to the discussion of the reunion movement in view of which the bridge-theory was evolved.   There are,
however, a number of questions still remaining which deal with
the internal life of the Church of England, and we must first
examine these so that we may have a more complete picture of
Anglicanism as it really is.   A knowledge of Anglican faith and
practice will help us to a fuller realization of the issues involved
in the reunion of the churches.

NOTES TO CHAPTER II

(1) A. S. Duncan Jones, in Williams and Harris, *Northern
Catholicism,* p. 444.

(2) H. E. Symonds, *The Council of Trent and Anglican
Formularies,* p. x, note.

(3) G. K. A. Bell, *Randall Davidson,* p. 1111 note.

(4) H. N. Bate (Editor), *Faith and Order, Lausanne, 1927,* p. 337.

(5) Bell, *Documents,* i. 90-1.

(6) Z. N. Brooke, *The English Church and the Papacy.*   F.
Dvornik, *National Churches and the Church Universal,* p.
57, says of Brooke's work :   ' his findings   .   .   . will for
long remain classical.'

(7) L. O'Donovan, (editor), *Assertio Septem Sacramentorum,*
p. 189. (translation ours).

(8) K. D. Mackenzie, *The Confusion of the Churches,* p. 75.
See also G. D. Rosenthal, in Mackenzie, *Union of Christendom,* i. 68.

(9) G. F. Holden, *The Special Bases of the Anglican Claim,*
p. 186.

(10) Holden, op. cit., p. 173. This writer gives an excellent exposition of the theological justification for nationality in religion on p. 168 ff. We have nothing to quarrel with in this. We deny, however, the continued assumption by the author that he is arguing a thesis denied by the Catholic Church, as he says explicitly on p. 6 when speaking of nationality: ' Perhaps there is no point on which the Church of England comes more sharply into collision with Rome than this.'

(11) Bell, *Randall Davidson*, p. 797. H. Johnson, *Anglicanism in Transition*, p. 163, speaks of the Establishment party which Newman said was ' more eager that there should be a National Church than careful what that National Church professes.'

(12) K. D. Mackenzie, *The Confusion of the Churches*, p. 15.

(13) T. S. Eliot, *Selected Essays*, p. 371.

(14) C. P. S. Clarke, *The Via Media*, pp. 7-8.

(15) T. M. Parker, in Mackenzie, *Union of Christendom*, i. 202.

(16) Quoted in *The Times*, November, 8, 1949.

(17) J. W. C. Wand, in Mackenzie, *Union of Christendom*, ii. 6.

(18) H. Rashdall, *Christus in Ecclesia*, p. 329.

(19) *Tract 90*, p. 82.

(20) Messenger, *The Reformation, The Mass, and the Priesthood*, ii. 298.

(21) W. A. Visser t'Hooft, *Anglo-Catholicism and Orthodoxy : A Protestant View*, p. 24.

(22) A. R. Vidler, *Witness to the Light* (The Theology of F. D. Maurice), p. 217.

(23) Bell, *Randall Davidson*, p. 1158.

(24) A. G. Hebert, *The Form of the Church*, p. 100.

(25) H. L. Goudge, *The Church of England and Reunion*, p. 316.

(26) D. T. Jenkins, *The Nature of Catholicity*, p. 155.

(27) C. P. S. Clarke, op. cit., p. 187.

(28) L. Hodgson (Ed.) *The Doctrine of the Church* etc. p. 29.

(29) *The Conversations at Malines 1921-1925*, p. 12.

(30) Eliot, op. cit., p. 369.

(31) L. Walker, S. J., *The Problem of Reunion*, p. 49.

(32) Quoted in t'Hooft, op. cit., p. 11.

CHAPTER III

ANGLICAN FAITH AND PRACTICE

It is difficult to get a correct picture of the religious life of the Church of England to-day. We hear frequently of the Catholic ceremonial that is gradually being introduced by Anglo-Catholics, and we are impressed by the Lambeth Conference with its grand total of over three hundred bishops. Despite these outward appearances, however, it is becoming clearer every day that the Church of England has failed to retain the loyalty of the great majority of the English people, and that it is at present only a vast organization with relatively few active members.

That indifferentism has captured the masses in England to-day is generally admitted. Professor Joad draws a grim picture of what he calls the 'drift from the Churches,'[1] and it is admitted that the shortage of clergy has become so critical as to endanger seriously the parochial system of the Church of England. Further, ever since the re-awakening of Catholic tendencies by the Oxford Movement, the number of Anglicans turning to the Church of Rome has been steadily increasing, and the ' path to Rome, once narrow and stony for Anglican converts, has broadened into an arterial road, crowded with fashionable company.'[2] Although it cannot be said, perhaps, that this annual loss affects the Church of England very much numerically, yet intellectually and spiritually it represents a tremendous impoverishment of the church these converts leave, for they always include some of the best minds in Anglicanism.

The parallel is an interesting one between the theological definition of membership which we have examined in Chapter I and the actual membership of the Church of England as it stands to-day. According as the definition of membership becomes wider and more vague, the actual membership becomes less. Some writers would see not merely a parallel but a causal connection between the two movements, implying that making membership less exacting makes it something less worth while, and thereby members are lost. Thus Father Ronald Knox writes : ' It appears, then, that the two processes are going on side by side, the decline of Church membership and the decline of dogma,' and he goes on to show that the decline of dogma generally is at least partly responsible for the decline in membership. ([3]) Whether or not we agree with this line of reasoning, the absence of any clearly-defined and easily recognizable teaching in the Church of England seems to be at least one of the causes of the failure of that church to-day.

We have already examined the comprehensiveness of the Church of England in the matter of dogmatic belief, and we have shown that one of the main causes of that comprehension lies in the spirit of nationalism to which the Church of England is committed. It is indeed conceivable that a national church could, in theory at least, possess a clear and definite system of doctrine and impose it on the whole nation. For such a system to be successful, however, a central authority would have to exist, capable of deciding defini-tively on matters of belief and interpreting the received body of teaching as the need might arise. The absence of such an authority in the Church of England is, we hope to show, at least a con-tributory cause in the general process of ' watering down ' of doctrine which is so marked in the last fifty years.

The first and most obvious question about authority in the Church of England is this : What authority does the Church of England itself possess ? Is that church the infallible teacher of divine truth, and is it ever ready to settle disputes which may arise on matters of faith ? The answer to this question is quite definite : the Church of England does not look upon itself as an infallible teaching body. Some would allow that infallibility and indefectibility belong to the ' Universal Church,' and Article XX of the Thirty-nine Articles tells us that the church has ' authority in controversies of faith,' but on the other hand the Church of England does not claim to be anything more that a particular local church, and Article XIX tells us that such particular churches may err.

The 1938 report on Doctrine in the Church of England give us an interesting examination of the question of the authority of the church. It begins with a statement which might be found in a Catholic work of theology :

> The authority of the Church in the realm of doctrine arises from its commission to preach the Gospel to all the world, and the promises, accompanying that commission, that the Lord would always be with His disciples and that the Holy Spirit would guide them into all the truth. ([4])

As a declaration of the existence of a divinely-appointed and divinely-guarded magisterium, this paragraph is precise and orthodox. The following sentences, however, withdraw and positively contradict everything that this first sentence has enunciated, and we come eventually to a declaration of the Lutheran principle of private judgment as the ultimate rule of faith. The whole section is an interesting one, but here we must confine ourselves to a short summary of the stages by which this fundamental change is brought about in the report. The following propositions give the general tenor of the argument :

(i) The church's authoritive declaration must be interpreted as resting, at least partly, on the free and continuous *consensus fidelium ;*

(ii) Doctrines 'which the Church has been generally united in teaching' must be allowed 'very high authority,' yet one who feels bound in conscience to reject them may do so;

(iii) Each individual should test and check the church's doctrine as far as he can, and should 'think out his own belief.'

By admitting the last of these propositions, the Doctrinal Commission has completely contradicted its introductory paragraph on the church's magisterium. The acceptance of private judgment as the final court of appeal destroys entirely the notion of an *ecclesia docens.* It excludes not merely an *infallible* teaching authority, but also such a fallible one as most Anglicans would admit the church to be. If a man can pit his private judgment against the authority of the church, then that church, be it fallible or infallible, is quite useless to him *as a teacher*. Despite the report's clear statement that the church possesses authority in the realm of doctrine, we are here told that private judgment is the ultimate criterion of faith.

Although Anglican theologians generally would not subscribe to the teaching put forward in this section of the report, the principles they enunciate lead ultimately to the same conclusion. For Bishop Gore, the doctrine of authority as expounded in the Catholic Church involves an abdication of reason in those who accept it, and the only form of authority that we can allow to the church is that it should teach people the truths of the Christian faith, but that as soon as possible the individual must turn to the bible, 'to deepen, develop, verify, purge his faith by the study of the Scripture.'([5]) The same view of the church as a merely human teacher — or as something slightly better, but still liable to make mistakes — is defended at length by Salmon, who compares the church to a town clock, normally authoritative but still liable to error,([6]) and is also accepted by A. J. Carlyle who declares that questions of faith cannot be settled once and for all by invoking the authority of the church, for 'the church must justify itself by its conformity with the norm of the teaching of our Lord.'([7]) These and other Anglican theologians who hold the same view would logically have to admit that the authority of the church as they conceive it must ultimately yield place to private judgment as the final criterion of revealed truth.

Since we cannot find in the teaching-office of the Church of England that authority which is necessary in matters of faith, we must look elsewhere for this authority. Many Anglican writers point to the official formularies of the Church of England as being the final court of appeal. These formularies are the Thirty-nine Articles, the Book of Common Prayer, and to a less extent the Ordinal. We have already examined the Articles from the point of view of their doctrinal content, and here we are interested only in the authority they possess. Whatever might be said of the authority of the Articles in earlier days, it is made quite clear that they have no real authority in the Church of England to-day. Since 1865 the assent which the clergy have to give to them is merely a 'general' assent.   It is clear from recent Anglican writings that this 'general' assent is quite compatible with complete rejection of the doctrinal content of the Articles.   'If we can sincerely say,' remarks Dr. Goudge, 'that we are neither Unitarians, nor Pelagians, nor Anabaptists, nor Roman Catholics, few are likely to quarrel with us for giving our "assent" to the Articles.'(8) The 1938 report on Anglican doctrine, intent as usual on pleasing both sides, says first that the Articles and other for-mularies still define the position of the Church of England in relation to other Churches, but it is careful to add that they must not be allowed to prejudge modern questions, and it foresees the rejection of some of these formularies by Anglican theologians.

The authority of the Book of Common Prayer cannot be defined independently of the authority of the Articles, and party attach-ments again decide the question.   For the High Church party, the Articles must be interpreted in the light of the Prayer Book, while for the Low Church the Protestant interpretation of the Articles comes first, and the Prayer Book must be interpreted in the light of this.   It is interesting to discover a difference of opinion on this precise point among the members of the Anglican delegation in the discussions with the Old Catholic Churches, the Anglo-Catholic and Evangelical members being unable to agree on the authority of the Articles and the Prayer Book in relation to one another.

Just as the arrangement of 'general assent' to the Articles has successfully taken from them all dogmatic authority and made them a document of purely historical interest, so too any authority the Prayer Book may have possessed has been done away with, though much less easily than in the case of the Articles.   Almost since the beginning of the present century a revision of the Prayer Book was being planned.   Called the 'Deposited Book,' it was in-troduced into Parliament in 1927 and again in 1928, and was both times rejected.   It was, however, printed as a private book and permission to use it in the Church of England was given in 1929. Thus although in strict theory the Prayer Book of 1662 is still in force, the last vestige of its authority has been swept away by the wide-spread use of the Deposited Book.

We need not delay over the assent to be given to the Ordinal; in practice it is merely an act of faith in the validity of Anglican

Orders and does not affect the question of authority. Our conclusion must therefore be that the Anglican formularies which we
have examined do not possess any real authority in matters of faith.
They are at best documents of purely historical interest and have
no bearing on the faith of the Church of England to-day.

To one reading the resolutions and reports of the various Lambeth Conferences it might appear that these Conferences are
gradually becoming authoritative councils for the whole Anglican
Communion. The 1930 Conference declared that 'at the present
time the Lambeth Conference is the visible bond which unites the
different portions of the Anglican Communion to one another.' If
it is the visible bond which unites the various Anglican churches,
one would think that it should possess some authority consistent
with that function. Further, the definitive way in which decisions
on matters of faith and morals are given would lead us to believe
that the Conference is the official magisterium for the Anglican
world.

That the Lambeth Conference is not a legislative synod and
that it has no power beyond the moral influence of its decisions
themselves is a truth which is frequently brought to our notice
in the Conferences. Before Archbishop Longley convoked the
first Lambeth Conference in 1867 he said that he would refuse to
convene any assembly which would pretend to make decisions
binding the church. That tradition has been faithfully adhered to
in the Conferences which have been held up to the present. Thus
the 1948 report says that earlier Conferences have wisely rejected
suggestions for a legislative synod, and the booklet *Lambeth and
You,* discussing the question of the authority of the Conference's
findings, says that they have 'only the authority of the bishops
assembled at Lambeth,' and adds that if it be necessary to give
definite authority to any particular section of the report, individual bishops or churches can do so. The Lambeth Conferences,
then, have no real authority either for the Anglican Communion
as a whole, or, what is more directly to our purpose, for the
Church of England.

If the bishops of the Anglican Communion, solemnly gathered
together to discuss and decide on questions of faith and morals,
have no authority to impose their decisions, we may well ask :
what is the authority of the individual bishop in his own diocese ?

Despite the traditional Anglican reverence for the episcopal office, the bishop has no real power to-day even within the confines of his own territory. This was abundantly proved in the various liturgical and doctrinal disputes which broke out all over England at the beginning of the present century, and even to the present day bishops find themselves unable to take effective action against their own subjects who refuse to abide by the liturgical and doctrinal formularies generally accepted. The outstanding example is the 'Reservation' dispute, where Anglican bishops found their authority openly flouted by Anglo-Catholics with 'Roman' ideas on the subject of the Real Presence. On the other hand, it is perhaps fortunate that bishops of the Church of England have no authority in matters of doctrine, as the teaching of men like Bishop Barnes of Birmingham and Bishop Henson of Hereford (and later of Durham), if imposed on their dioceses, might destroy the last vestiges of Christian faith in their subjects. Further, part of the price to be paid for Anglican participation in reunion schemes is to be, if we may use the word, the 'constitutionalization' of the episcopate. This will mean in practice that presbyters will in future share more of the powers of the bishops (to suit Presbyterians), and the congregation will take a large share in the running of the diocese (to suit Congregationalists). This lowering of the bishop's remaining authority is taken so far in the new Church of South India that the laity can over-rule the bishops even in questions of the faith and practice of the church.

A new departure was made in this question of the authority of bishops in the discussions with the Eastern Orthodox delegation which attended the Lambeth Conference of 1930. The Orthodox delegation, weary of discussing questions of doctrine with committees which had no authority to decide on them, asked the plain blunt question : 'What is the supreme constitutional body in the Anglican Church which decides authoritatively in the matter of differences of faith ?' Obviously an answer had to be found on the Anglican side which would be acceptable to the Orthodox — an answer which would if possible agree with the teaching of the Orthodox Churches on the source of authority. And so the Anglicans replied that ' in matters of doctrine the final and governing decision, as well as the final statement of the point at issue, lay with the House of Bishops.' We must question both the sincerity and the truth of this statement, for it is unthinkable that the House of Bishops of the Church of England should agree to issue a definitive declaration on a disputed question of faith. They have not done so in the past, and it is extremely unlikely that they will do so in the future. We cannot avoid the conclusion that this statement made to the Orthodox was framed solely in order to satisfy the Eastern Churches and does not at all correspond to the situation which exists in the Church of England to-day.

We need not discuss the possibility of a General Council being the source of authority in matters of faith for the Church of England. The teaching of the Councils of the undivided church is of course accepted, but that is so only because 'they satisfy the Christian consciousness, and they correspond with the experience of the whole church.' The 1938 report on doctrine in the Church of England says the same thing when it tells us that the authority of these councils rests in part at least on the *consensus* of Christendom. In any case the teaching of Article XXI is clear in its repudiation of the authority of General Councils : 'Generalia Concilia . . . et errare possunt, et interdum errarunt etiam in his quae ad Deum pertinent.' (General Councils . . . can err, and have sometimes erred, even in those things which relate to God).

One of the central doctrines of the continental Reformation was the claim that private interpretation of scripture was the ultimate rule of faith. Article VI of the Thirty-nine Articles is very close to this teaching and says that 'Holy Scripture containeth all things necessary to salvation,' and Article XX says further that it is not lawful for the church to ordain anything contrary to God's word. If we take these two Articles at their face value, then scripture is prior to the church, and the authority of the church is completely subject to the authority of the written word.

The Catholic attitude to this question is clear. It is pointed out that once you make the church's authority a secondary thing you have no guarantee that the scriptures are inspired — you do not even know what books are contained in scripture, for it is only the church can tell you this. Anglican theology, aware of the force of this objection, has never fully decided whether the church or the scriptures come first, and is content to place the two side by side without defining their relation to one another. That is really the position taken up in the Articles, for despite these protestations of the superiority of scripture the same Article (XX) tells us, as we have noted elsewhere, that the church has authority in controversies of faith.

In an interesting booklet, D. T. Jenkins, a Barthian Protestant writer, takes up the position that the Church of England is officially committed to teaching the priority of the scriptures to the church, and must therefore be prepared to accept the Barthian principle of 'Reformation according to the word of God.' He shows that the acceptance of that principle, which he claims to be the only test of catholicity, will clear away all obstacles in the way of reunion with the continental Reformed Churches.

Against this line of argument the Anglican theologian has only one defence, namely, to deny the absolute priority and supremacy of scripture, and to fall back, in some measure at least, on the authority of the church. We have already seen that he does not allow any independent authority to the church, and here we find that he cannot allow any independent authority to the scriptures. The dilemma is inescapable — either the Church or scripture. To accept the church as primary is to be Catholic and means the repudiation of the Reformation ; to accept the scriptures as primary is to be Protestant. There is no via media.

The Church of England is an 'Established' church in the full sense of the word — that is, it is constituted by the law of the state and is, theoretically at least, subject to the civil power in all things. In the sixteenth century the position did not appear anomalous, as all the members of parliament belonged to the national church. In the present century, however, it was felt that this situation could not be tolerated as at least half the members of parliament do not belong to the Church of England. After some agitation the 'Enabling Act' was passed in 1919, and this gave a certain amount of real freedom to the church. It was felt that once the National Assembly had expressed the opinion of the whole church on any given question, Parliament would not oppose its wishes. These hopes were doomed to disappointment. We have already noted briefly the rejection of the Deposited Book in 1927 and again in 1928. This revision of the Book of Common Prayer was intended to give a wide range of services while at the same time insisting that the range was limited, and did not allow 'Roman' practices like High Mass or general 'Reservation' as adopted in most Anglo-Catholic churches. Despite this anti-Roman attitude of the book, many concessions were made in favour of Anglo-Catholic liturgical practices, and these were seized upon by the Low Church party. The introduction of an epiclesis in the Eucharist and the formulation of a rite for the communion of the sick were taken as implying transubstantiation. After heated debates the House of Commons rejected the proposed changes, and it is noticeable that the votes which condemned the book came mainly from non-Anglicans — members for Northern Ireland, Scotland, Wales and from others who were not belong to the Church of England at all.

The implications of this rejection are far-reaching. It showed that ultimately the Church of England is ruled by a lay body composed mainly of non-Anglicans, and that this body has power not merely in the secular side of the church's life, but in matters of liturgy, discipline and doctrine. The rejection shows, too, the deep-seated fear of Rome that exists in the English mind — Archbishop Davidson's comment was that 'there is no force on earth so determined and uncompromising as the force of the No-Popery cry in England.'[9] The idea of printing the Deposited Book as an ordinary book was a brilliant one, and the American writer Horton says that it undoubtedly saved the Church of England from breaking up as a result of this crisis.[10] The result is that any congregation which desires the proposed changes may use the Deposited Book. We are informed that it is being used widely in the Church of England, and parliament has apparently taken no steps to press the issue.

In the foregoing pages we have examined several sources of authority in the Church of England with a view to ascertaining their exact relation to one another. Leaving aside the intervention of parliament, which is most exceptional, we can state that of the sources which we have examined, there is not one which is generally admitted by Anglicans themselves to be supreme. Different writers proclaim different sources of authority, and we are left with the general impression that there is no real authority in the Church of England. In this state of theological doubt it was almost inevitable that some one should eventually suggest that while no one source of authority was supreme, a combination of many or even of all the sources provided a form of authority sufficiently coherent and unified to claim the allegiance of the whole church. The enunciation of this theory is to be found in one of the committee reports of the 1948 Lambeth Conference. We are first given the statement of the difficulty :

> The question is often asked, "Is Anglicanism based on a sufficiently coherent form of authority to form the nucleus of a world-wide fellowship of Churches, or does its comprehensiveness conceal internal divisions which may cause its disruption ?"

Having thus disarmed the would-be objector, the report proposes the solution that, while authority in the Anglican Communion is single in that it is derived from a single divine source, it is nevertheless

> distributed among Scripture, Tradition, Creeds, the Ministry of the Word and Sacraments, the witness of saints, and the *consensus fidelium* . . . It is thus a dispersed rather that a centralised authority having many elements which combine, interact with, and check each other; these elements together contributing by a process of mutual support, mutual checking, and redressing of errors or exaggerations to the many-sided fullness of the authority which Christ has committed to His Church.

Having thus stated its belief in the nature of authority, the committee proceeds in the following paragraphs to list its virtues. It has 'suppleness' and 'elasticity'; it is 'simple and intelligible'; it has its different elements 'in organic relation to each other,' and what is most important, it is 'essentially Anglican.' We are left with the impression that the whole treatment is insincere, especially when we recall that the 1930 Conference told the Orthodox Delegation that the House of Bishops was the supreme authority in matters of faith in the Church of England. We can hardly believe that the Church of England has changed its form of authority so drastically in the short space of eighteen years, and we are not unfair, I think, when we conclude that the distributing of authority over so many sources is an implicit admission that there is no real authority in matters of faith in the Church of England.

That this lack of authority can give rise to many problems is fully realised by Anglican theologians, but they seem to be quite satisfied with the position provided their freedom is assured in the matter of religious belief.   Since the affair of the Jerusalem bishopric in the last century, there have been many serious crises in the Church of England, and during at least two of these — the disputes about Modernism and the Deposited Book — it looked almost certain that the church was going to split in two.   That this is always a possibility in the Church of England is freely admitted.   Thus S. C. Carpenter notes that 'unity in diversity' is one of the mottoes of Anglicanism and comments that while the diversity is often bewildering the unity is sometimes seriously threatened.(11)   Sheila Kaye-Smith confesses that 'one of the stimulating conditions of being an Anglican is that you never know what is going to happen next — you cannot feel confident that there might not be some sudden betrayal.'(12)   Despite these protestations, we find in Anglican theology a quiet confidence that the Church of England will somehow overcome all its difficulties, and a belief that no crisis however serious will succeed in dividing a church in which such wide freedom is tolerated.   If, however, a schism occurs in the Church of England, it will almost certainly be on the question of authority.

It is not at all likely that any effort will be made in the future to set up a central authority in matters of doctrine, though the earlier Lambeth Conferences were very anxious that one should be set up.   Thus the 1867 Conference suggested the appointment of a voluntary spiritual tribunal which might act as a court of appeal in doctrinal disputes, and the 1888 Conference went a step further in demanding 'a plain and brief summary of the definite doctrinal grounds upon which the Anglican Churches stand.' Nothing was done, however, to implement these suggestions, but special circumstances caused the publication fifty years later of a document which might be taken to satisfy the request of the Conference of 1888.   We refer to the 1938 report on doctrine, to which we must now turn.

Christopher Dawson has shown that it is oddly paradoxical that the movement which began in Oxford in 1833 should within a century have turned into a complete denial of what that movement

stood for. The Tractarians defended authority as against Liberalism, while to-day the Anglo-Catholic movement has accepted
Liberalism, and is threatened with a complete surrender to the
modernist group.([13])

In order to understand properly the situation as it arose in
the Church of England, we must clearly distinguish two elements
in modernism. The first of these is Liberalism, or a sceptical
attitude to the received doctrine of the church in view of the
results of modern historical research. The second element is that
which alone truly merits the name of modernism, and may best be
summed up as the acceptance of immanentist philosophy in religion.
The two elements are normally found together, and were found
together in modernism as it appeared in the Catholic Church, but
nevertheless the distinction is absolutely necessary in view of the
developments in the Church of England.

Liberalism seems to have entered the Oxford Movement almost
when Newman left it, and the famous work *Essays and Reviews,*
published in 1860, is quite as liberal as anything that has ever
appeared in English theological writing. It is also noteworthy
that the Lambeth Conference of 1888 requested the Archbishop of
Canterbury to ascertain whether it be desirable to revise the
English version of the creeds. Modernism in the second sense of
belief in immanentist philosophy did not take root fully in Anglican
theology until after the publication of the decree 'Lamentabili' and
the encyclical 'Pascendi,' both of which condemned modernism in
the Catholic Church in 1907.

The distinction which we have just made between the two
elements in modernism applies first and foremost to the Catholic
von Hügel. Without some account of him, no study of modernism
in England would be complete, for his influence on Anglicans
generally was immense and is admitted everywhere. In doctrine
he accepted fully the destructive liberal views of the Abbé Loisy
while at the same time repudiating in theory at least the immanentist philosophy that was part of the whole modernist movement.
He did not realize, of course, that the acceptance of Loisy's
conclusions led directly either to scepticism or to immanentism.
His influence on Anglicans arose from a combination of many
elements — his acceptance of Loisy's teaching and his professed
hatred for the Roman Curia, coupled with his insistence that

this, and this only, is true Catholicism. He thus summed up for Anglicans that 'Liberal Catholicism' which was to find its greatest exponent in one who acknowledged his very great debt to von Hügel's teaching — Bishop Charles Gore, with whose life the modernist struggle in England is completely entwined.

Bishop Gore's position in Anglican theology is one that is easy to sympathize with, if difficult to defend. It centred around three points which historical circumstances more than anything else forced Gore to combine into a system. These three central beliefs of his teaching were liberalism, anti-modernism, and Fundamentalism. Here we are concerned mainly with the first two and the strange fact of their presence in one theological system. Unlike von Hügel, Gore seemed to realize that Liberalism in theology was destructive of the very foundations of faith, and while he wished to have a certain amount of liberalism in his theology, he intended that liberalism to have very definite limits. His opponents not unfairly retorted that if you accept the principles of liberalism at all, you must follow them to their logical conclusion.

The liberal side of Gore's teaching appeared mostly in his earlier works. In *Lux Mundi,* which he edited in 1889, his own essay amounted to a denial of the principle of scriptural inspiration, and his Bampton Lectures two years later accepted a mitigated form of kenoticism. With the turn of the century, however, he seems to have realized the ravages that were being caused by the denial of the traditional meaning of the creeds, and from 1911 he pressed for a condemnation of modernism in the Church of England in some such form as the papal condemnations of 1907. A temporary agreement was reached of the question of modernism in 1912, but trouble arose again in 1917 when a leading modernist, Canon Hensley Henson, was appointed bishop of Hereford. Gore entered a formal protest against the nomination on the ground that Henson in his published works had denied the reality of Christ's resurrection. From this time two dogmas became an obsession with Gore — the Resurrection and the Virgin Birth. At every turn he put them forward as test of orthodoxy, and to the end of his life they appear everywhere in his writings as doctrines that must be accepted in the strict literal sense. In practically every one of his works he attacked modernism in all its forms. Thus he wrote in 1918 : 'All so-called progress which takes us away from the firm standing-ground of the apostolic faith, is not progress but loss.'([14])   In his later works he is equally definite and explicit in his repudiation of modernist principles.

In 1919 Bishop Gore resigned the see of Oxford, his main reason being his belief that he could defend the historical inter-pretation of the creeds better with his pen than with episcopal authority.   The immediate occasion of his resignation was not the modernist question but the decision of the Representative Church Council that baptism alone — not Confirmation — be required for membership of the future Church Assembly.   The modernist dis-pute however was certainly the main cause.   Dr. Prestige, his biographer, writes of the resignation that it was brought on mainly by exhaustion at his efforts to move the other bishops to act against modernism, which most of them believed to be wrong, but their 'misconceived and mischievous idea of toleration' had left him to fight the battle alone.([15])

The resignation of Bishop Gore did not solve the difficulty. The enthusiasm displayed in the 'Appeal to all Christian People' of the 1920 Lambeth Conference diverted people's attention for the moment from the more fundamental question of the creeds, which Archbishop Davidson had refused a place on the agenda of the Conference.   In 1921 a paper read by the leading modernist Hastings Rashdall at the Conference of Modern Churchmen caused another storm of protest in which Gore again took a leading part.   Eventually Davidson agreed to the setting up of a Com-mission — 'a time-honoured expedient' — with the terms of reference :

> To consider the nature and grounds of Christian doctrine with a view to demonstrating the extent of existing agree-ment within the Church of England and with a view to investigating how far it is possible to remove or diminish existing differences.

The report of the commission did not appear until 1938.([16]) In the meantime, the heat of controversy had died down, and what was more important, Bishop Gore was dead.   Nevertheless, the reception given to the report shows that Gore's struggle had not been entirely in vain.   Over 8,000 of the clergy of the Church of

England presented a protest against the purely symbolic interpretation of the creeds as set forth in the report. Dr. Mitchell lists the spirited reactions of the various bodies in the Church of England,([17]) and it looked as if the controversy might be renewed again, but the two Convocations passed resolutions merely 'recommending the Doctrinal Report to the attention of the Church,' and refusing to imply acceptance or rejection of the doctrine contained in it. This was fully in harmony with Davidson's wishes in appointing the Commission, namely that the Report should be laid before the bishops to see what further action they should take, 'if any.'

The official High Church commentary on the Report was drawn up by Fr. A. G. Hebert and published in 1939 under the title *Memorandum on the Report of the Archbishop's Commission*. Its main criticisms may be classed under three headings : (i) the report allows 'an undefined fluidity of belief'; (ii) it positively denies fundamental dogmas and — (iii) it was out of date when it appeared. With all three of these criticisms we can fully concur. Under the different headings in the report all the possible variations of belief are listed, and the Commission allows complete freedom of choice — a choice which is, in the words of a Catholic commentator, 'as embarrassing as the choice of services, or of methods of conducting the same service, offered to clergymen in the "Deposited Book." '([18]) When it deals with the central dogmas of Christianity it deprives them of their historical basis, and we note especially the purely modernist treatment of Gore's two watchwords — the Virgin-Birth and the Ressurrection. We can hardly imagine such a report being issued during Gore's lifetime.

What is most striking, however, is Fr. Hebert's attitude to the modernism of the report. Even a casual reading of the first hundred pages of the text of the report should convince anyone that we have there modernism in its most advanced form, either officially propounded or at least tolerated. Yet Fr. Hebert affects to be surprised that there should be so little modernism in the document. He writes : 'The Report in fact appears to mark a decisive stage in the retreat from Modernism ; indeed, in a cool hour the significant thing about this Report will be seen to be the extent to which the distinctively Modernist positions have

been given up.'([19])   Later he repeats the assertion that it is a
retreat from modernism.   Fr. Hebert seems to forget, however, that
the title of the report which he is reviewing is not *Doctrine in
the Modernist Party*, but *Doctrine in the Church of England*.
The report was put forward seriously by the Commission as an
account of the existing agreements and disagreements in the Church
of England and we should naturally expect that the doctrine contained in it should be fairly representative of the whole church.
When Fr. Hebert admits that the report of this Commission is
a 'retreat from Modernism', he is admitting the full extent to which
modernist teaching has penetrated Anglican thought to-day at
all levels.

Our main interest in the report is its treatment of the doctrine
of the church. It deals twice with this subject — first briefly,
as a source of authority, and later at greater length under the
heading 'The Church and Sacraments.'   We have already discussed the treatment given to the question of authority in the
church and have found it inconsistent.([20])   The second treatment
is no less unsatisfactory.   The modernist complacency about the
divisions in Christendom, noted above, is again present here :
'the life of the Christian Body is enriched by varieties of emphasis
and interpretation, and historically these have been developed in
their familiar forms in the several communions which have resulted
from the divisions in the Church.'([21])   The note of unity is
interpreted as belonging to the future church and not to the
actual church, and schism is defined as a division within the Christian Body.   And finally, we can never be quite sure during most
of the discussion whether the Commission is speaking of the visible
or of the invisible church.

That such a report could be accepted in the Church of England
is an alarming symptom of the attitude of that church to revealed
truth.   Bishop Gore's life was the only real protest against the
introduction of modernist principles, and to-day the protests are
very few.   Modernism has found in the Church of England the
home that was denied to it in the Catholic Church.   In 1909
George Tyrrell wrote : 'Possibly the Church of England may be
able to accept the results of history, and yet retain the substance
of her Catholicism, i.e. she may have room for Modernism   .   .   .
If Modernism fails in the Church of England, it may be abandoned

as a noble dream.' (²²) Of the triumph of Modernism in the Church of England there can be no longer any doubt. Christopher Dawson sees only two possibilities — a complete return to Catholic intellectual principles or a further union with Liberal Protestantism resulting in what he calls 'the amorphous unity of a creedless undenominationalism.' (²³)

The connection between faith and morals has always been a close one, and the absence of a responsible authority in matters of faith is bound to have its effects on the standard of morals. Here we wish to examine one particular case in which the Lambeth Conferences have given very definite, if inconsistent, teaching, and it may, I think, be taken as an indication of the general attitude to questions of ethics which exists in the Anglican Communion. The earlier Conferences took up the Catholic position on the question of contraception, and some of their condemnations of the practice are quite as vehement as any condemnations issued by the Catholic Church. The Conference of 1897 says that 'the verdict of Nature appears to endorse the moral instinct which condemns these practices,' and suggests that the increase of insanity may be closely connected with them. The next Conference, held eleven years later, uses even stronger language and goes so far as to pass three resolutions on contraception, which it declares to be 'demoralizing to character and hostile to national welfare.' The 1920 Conference followed the same teaching and issued an emphatic warning against the grave dangers incurred by those using unnatural means for the avoidance of conception.

Despite these continued rejections of illicit birth-control, the Conference of 1930 fully authorised the use of contraception. In a resolution which was passed by 193 votes to 67, the bishops declared : 'In those cases where there is such a clearly-felt moral obligation to limit or avoid parenthood, and where there is a morally sound reason for avoiding complete abstinence, the Conference agrees that other methods may be used.' It was one of the very rare occasions on which a resolution was not passed in the normal form of 'nem.con.', and the fact that the minority refused to withdraw its opposition shows that some at least of those voting realized the tragic nature of the resolution.

This resolution on birth-control is the one outstanding factor in the 1930 Conference. The pages upon pages of discussions on the reunion of the churches are entirely eclipsed by it, and it is the one feature by which the 1930 Conference will be known in history. For Bishop Gore it was the last straw. He had conducted the retreat in preparation for the Conference, and he never imagined that such a decision was possible. His biographer says that it 'reduced him to indignation and almost to despair.'[24] He tried to organize a crusade against it, but the resolution was a popular one and could not be resisted. T. S. Eliot wrote that the Conference 'was right and courageous to express a view on the subject of procreation radically different from that of Rome,'[25] and we may well believe that the anti-Roman flavour of the decision did not make it anything less popular in the churches of the Anglican Communion. The 1958 Conference shows the inevitable consequences of the 1930 decision : a learned theological defence of contraception, acceptance of A.I.H., and a blessing for voluntary sterilization, provided the decision is made "in deepest and most conscientious thought."

In treating of the Anglican attitude to morality, much might be said in connection with the teaching of the Church of England on the nature and properties of marriage. Despite the official acceptance of marriage as a life-long contract, there is complete toleration of divorce and remarriage, and this is clearly brought out in the permission given for a 'private form of prayer and dedication' on the occasion of the remarriage of divorced persons. Such a union is regarded as valid and lawful, and the parties can be admitted to the Eucharist at the discretion of the bishop. The Conference of 1948 in setting forth these regulations was explicitly contradicting a principle laid down at the previous Conference, and its Committee had to agree to a 'difference of theological opinion' on whether the Matthean Exception (Matt. xix, 9) justifies the breaking of the marriage bond.

The question of authority is the central problem in any examination of Anglican theology. One can never be sure what exactly is the official teaching, nor how far the official teaching is accepted in practice. There is at times a complete refusal of subordination to any authority and an appeal to the 'freedom of the gospel.' With this attitude to authority it is impossible to argue or to refute. It shows, too, the real difficulty facing reunion schemes in which the Church of England is involved, namely, the impossibility of getting any one group which has a real claim to represent the whole church. If the negotiators agree to something which a particular group rejects, their authority as negotiators is repudiated. If the Church of England is so interested in reunion, it must be prepared to have some authority capable of acting on behalf of the whole church and not merely on behalf of certain sections of it. From the preceding pages it should be clear that it is quite unlikely that the Church of England will ever accept such an authority.

NOTES TO CHAPTER III

(1) C. E. M. Joad, *The Present and Future of Religion*, p. 11 ff.
(2) E. W. Barnes, *Should Such A Faith Offend ?*. p. 202
(3) Ronald Knox, *The Belief of Catholics*, p. 18 ff.
(4) *Doctrine in the Church of England*, p. 35.
(5) Gore, *The Incarnation of the Son of God*, p. 187.
(6) G. Salmon, *The Infallibility of the Church*, p. 114
(7) A. J. Carlyle, in *Contentio Veritatis*, p. 267.
(8) H. L. Goudge, *The Church of England and Reunion*, p. 316.
(9) Bell, *Randall Davidson*, p. 1354.
(10) W. M. Horton, *Contemporary English Theology*, p. 142.
(11) S. C. Carpenter, in Mackenzie, *Union of Christendom*, i. 301.
(12) Sheila Kaye-Smith, *Anglo-Catholicism*, p. 143.
(13) Christopher Dawson, *The Spirit of the Oxford Movement*, p. 134 ff. Dawson's analysis is accepted as correct by the Anglican, D. M. McKinnom, *The Church of God*, p. 87.
(14) C. Gore, *Dominant Ideas and Corrective Principles*, p. 25.
(15) G. L. Prestige, *Charles Gore*, p. 422.
(16) The report is entitled *Doctrine in the Church of England*.
(17) Rev. G. Mitchell, "Doctrine in the Church of England," in *I.E.R.*, 5th series, vol. ii, no. 4 (April 1938), p. 337 ff.
(18) H. J. T. Johnson, *Anglicanism in Transition*, p. 227.
(19) Hebert, *Memorandum*, p. 8.
(20) Supra, chapter II.
(21) *Doctrine in the Church of England*, p. 111 and see p. 107.
(22) Quoted in Vidler, *The Modernist Movement in the Roman Church*, p. 266.
(23) Dawson, op. cit., pp. 141-2.
(24) Prestige, *Charles Gore*, p. 515.
(25) T. S. Eliot, "Thoughts after Lambeth," in *Selected Essays*, p. 363.

CHAPTER IV

THE THEOLOGY OF REUNION

The theology of reunion is inevitably bound up with and based upon the theology of unity. To use the word reunion in the strict sense in relation to the church is to imply immediately that the church is not one to-day but is something divided which must be brought together. And so, for Catholics, since unity already exists, there is no such thing as the problem of reunion in the strict sense — there is only the problem of return. 'There is but one way,' wrote Pius XI, 'in which the unity of Christians may be fostered, and that is by furthering the return to the one true Church of Christ of those who are separated from it.'(1)

Once we leave the Catholic position, the theology of reunion undergoes a fundamental change, due almost entirely to the change in the meaning of unity. Despite the insistence on 'fundamental' and 'spiritual' unity which we have earlier discussed, there is everywhere an admission that the church to-day is, somehow or other, not one. There is, too, the recognition, though in some quarters it is not strong, that the church *should be* one. That is the problem of reunion as it is seen by non-Catholic eyes, and it is obvious that there can be many varieties of belief about it, since it depends on two variable quantities — firstly, as to how far the church is not one, and secondly as to how far it should be one. We have already discussed the first of these points briefly in our treatment of the unity of the church, and in the present chapter we shall examine the theological principles that are behind the modern efforts towards the realization of the second.

The reunion movement properly so called is something of very modern origin. There were, of course, many efforts in earlier centuries to heal the wounds caused by heresy and schism, and the work of the Council of Florence is especially well-known in this connection. It was only at the end of the last century, however, that the movement towards reunion began to be taken seriously and to assume the character of an orderly and systematic advance. Thus the first mention of reunion in the agenda of the Lambeth Conferences is found in the agenda for 1888 : 'The Anglican Communion in relation to the Eastern Churches, to the Scandinavian and other Reformed Churches, to the Old Catholics and others.' By the time of the next Conference (1897) reunion with the 'Latin Communion' found a place on the agenda. Since these two Conferences the question of reunion has tended to become the central and all-important item in the various Lambeth meetings.

Various explanations are put forward for this sudden interest in reunion. A common suggestion is that the so-called 'Catholic Revival' in the non-Roman churches has given rise to a greater realization of the doctrine of the church and of the consequent obligation of unity. Another, and perhaps more fundamental reason, is that the different sects, weary of continuous competition among themselves, are beginning to consider that co-operation might better their chances of survival. Their own failure as churches, and the corresponding success of the Catholic Church as seen especially on the mission-field is drawing the non-Catholic sects together — they are, as Fr. Knox writes, 'creeping closer to one another for warmth, in a world unresponsive to their message.'(²) The result is that to-day we are confronted with a large number of schemes of reunion and plans for closer co-operation between churches.

It was inevitable that the beginning of such a movement as this should be charcterized by many imprudent attempts at reunion and by much vague thinking on the subject of the church. The first impressions of the various parties seemed to be that all that was required was the will to unite, and it was presumed that all else would follow, but they soon found out that centuries of separation had crystallised, as it were, the very things that made them separate, and though there have been a number of reunions actually completed, it is generally admitted now that reunion will be a very slow and difficult process. The final reunion of all the churches is no longer seen as something just a few years away, but as a goal infinitely removed for which we are nevertheless bound to strive earnestly.

The literature on the reunion movement is already immense. Besides the books from individual writers there are a very great number of symposia in which writers of various communions discuss reunion from their own particular point of view. While these are of necessity of less value than books by individual authors, they are nevertheless helpful as giving us an idea as to how much a particular church is prepared to sacrifice for the cause of reunion. The reports of conferences held in view of reunion are especially valuable, as they show us reunion as it were *in fieri,* and they give a clear idea of what the parties believe the nature of the church to be. We shall confine ourselves to those efforts at reunion in which the Church of England has taken part.

The first question that must be asked in any discussion on reunion is this : What degree of union do the different churches seek ? Here the differences about the nature of unity make themselves felt immediately. The Free Churches, as we shall see, believe that the ideal situation exists when every congregation is absolutely independent of every other congregation, yet on good terms with everybody. Reunion for them means little more than becoming friendly with other congregations. Their attitude to real reunion is, like that of Catholics, a frank admission of *non possumus.* The Free Churches believe that 'wherever two or three are gathered together,' there is the church, and they hold that the unification of all these autonomous congregations into one organic whole is contrary to New Testament principles.

There is, however, one type of reunion, if we may call it reunion, which practically all, including the Free Churches, are willing to accept — the principle known as 'comity of missions.' This means that on the mission-field the different sects agree not to encroach on one another's territory where only one has already begun to make converts, or at least not to proselytize from one another where many are working together. The Catholic Church has, of course, always refused to recognise the principle of comity, and its missionaries have been unwilling to concentrate on any particular area while leaving other areas to non-Catholic denominations.

The acceptance of the principle of comity has far-reaching effects on the theology of reunion. It implies, first of all, a repudiation of exclusiveness, for a church which leaves a certain territory entirely to another religious body is admitting that the precept to preach the gospel to every creature is not addressed to itself exclusively. But comity does more than prevent over-lapping by Christian missionary bodies. It positively prepares the way for reunion for, in a territory where comity is in operation, when a Christian from one area enters a nearby area he will naturally be accepted as a Christian : to refuse to accept him as such would be to deny the principle of comity. Hence Bishop Newbigin rightly asserts that the acceptance of comity of missions was the beginning of the modern striving for unity,([3]) and it is very noticeable that schemes of reunion are progressing far more favourably in mission lands than in the countries which are providing the missionaries. The vast areas to be won for the gospel and the small means at their disposal have forced the different sects to do away with many of the barriers which divide them, and to unite for common action.

A step slightly higher than mere comity of missions is that type of reunion known as intercommunion. In the strict sense, this means that 'those who are communicants in the one body shall be privileged, on that ground alone, to be admitted to communion in the other body, without individual tests.' Intercommunion would therefore involve as a minimum the recognition by the various denominations of one another's ministry and sacraments, with particular reference to the Eucharist. It is difficult to see, however, whether the Church of England recognizes intercommunion as the final stage of reunion, or whether it is but the first of many steps towards corporate and organic reunion. In the 1930 Lambeth Conference we find it stated quite explicitly that intercommunion is the final stage : 'The Conference, maintaining as a general principle that intercommunion should be the goal of, rather than a means to the restoration of union . . .' This would agree partly with the teaching of the Orthodox Churches that intercommunion can be allowed only when complete dogmatic agreement has been reached between the churches. The Church of England will not of course demand complete dogmatic agreement as a condition of intercommunion.

If we accept intercommunion as the real goal of the reunion movement, we must be prepared to accept also the ideas of the universal church which it involves. It means that the universal church, having attained the ideal of unity, will consist of a large number of entirely autonomous national bodies, differing widely in matters of belief, yet united by common acceptance of the same sacraments, which thus constitute the only bond of unity between them. It would imply further that Christ never intended His church to consist of one organic unit, and it implies the rejection of schemes for corporate reunion as fanciful and unreal. The resulting unity would then be a mere federation such as the Free Churches already possess, and it would tolerate the use of the word 'church' in the strict sense for each of the bodies involved in the union.

Many Anglicans do not seem to require anything higher for the full realization of the ideals of the reunion movement. We can see immediately how intercommunion as a final goal fits in well with Anglican principles on unity, on membership, and on the church visible, which we have examined earlier. It guarantees too that the Anglican conception of the Church of England as a national church will not be lost as a price of reunion, and it promises full freedom to the principle of comprehensiveness. Finally, the Anglican hopes to see this unity coming as a result of the activities of his own church, the Bridge-Church.

Taken as a whole, then, the theory that intercommunion is the final goal of all reunion movement corresponds most closely to Anglican ideas about the church. If, as Anglicans tell us, the Church of England is to-day a miniature of what the united church will one day be, what greater bond of unity can that future church have than the 'intercommunion' which exists between the parties in the Church of England to-day? Outside of the Establishment, the only bond between a High Churchman and a Low Churchman is participation in the same sacraments, though even here their faith may be poles apart. To argue that the future universal church will be but an enlarged edition of the Church of England is in effect to make it a loose federation of independent bodies whose only unity is a sacramental one.

This ideal of the future church as merely universal intercommunion is not a high one, and hence we find many Anglicans paying at least lip-service to the highest form of unity — corporate reunion. To be satisfied with intercommunion is, writes the

Archbishop of Brisbane, 'a confession of essential disunion.'([4]) For Bishop Gore, corporate reunion was the only type of unity worth looking for, though he was realistic enough to admit that he could see no possibility of its speedy achievement.([5]) It is noteworthy too that the first Lambeth Conference which mentioned reunion suggested corporate reunion as the ultimate goal, as it said that the churches must be ready to consider what steps can be made towards corporate reunion or towards some intermediate stage which may prepare for it.

It must be admitted, I think, that the Church of England does not take the idea of corporate reunion seriously. In the negotiations with different churches the Anglican representatives in each case seemed to have no higher aim than to get an admission of the validity of Anglican orders and sacraments and an agreement of at least partial intercommunion with the other church. There is no consideration ever given to questions of corporate reunion, and we are led to the conclusion that if the Church of England has any interest in corporate reunion it is not an immediate interest. The sacrifices which that church would have to make with a view to corporate reunion would, it seems, be too great, and would perhaps interfere with that Anglican love of freedom and independence which caused the break with the Papacy. To enter into corporate reunion would interfere seriously with the principle of the autonomy of national churches, and there is perhaps a strong underlying fear that another papacy might arise as intolerable as the first.

The obstacles to all of the three types of reunion which we have mentioned are very great. Long years of separation have raised barriers of ignorance and prejudice between the churches, and it is recognized that the first real step to reunion is the clearing away of these. 'For the present, at least,' writes Dr. Swete, 'the hope of an approach to reunion lies not so much in the increase of organization . . . as the informal drawing together of the separated units of Christ's Body.'([6]) Further, each sect tends to value above all else that which it alone possesses, and in any scheme of reunion it will insist on making its own beliefs into a *conditio sine qua non*. As regards reunion with the Catholic Church, the main obstacle is the fact that the development of dogma has gone on as usual during the period when others were separated from her unity, and they find it impossible to accept developments which they claim to be accretions. The continued multiplication of smaller sects is an almost insuperable difficulty, for if reunionists are to be loyal to their own principles, they must include all these sects in their plans and give them representation at reunion conferences. In the Church of England itself the High Church party generally is aiming at union with Rome, while the Low Church is busy with approaches to the Free Churches, and thus threatening to disrupt the Church of England. In view of these and many other difficulties, it is generally admitted that reunion will be long in coming. Gore saw no prospect of reunion 'within the measurable future,' and long ago F. D. Maurice saw 'a convulsion far greater than that of the sixteenth century' on the road to reunion. Despite these warnings the believers in reunion are striving towards the realization of their ideal with a zeal which we cannot but admire, and every year brings information of new schemes proposed or completed in some part of the world.

The Lambeth Conference of 1920 will stand out in history as the great Conference of Reunion. It met at a time when the Church of England was in grave danger of breaking in two — 'in fear of deadlock, if not of schism.'[7] The heat of controversy over the Kikuyu affair had not yet died down,[8] and it was expected that Bishop Weston of Zanzibar would raise the matter again during the Conference. The modernist controversy was at its height, and Archbishop Davidson, as we have seen, had to make sure that the subject of the creeds would not appear on the agenda. To make matters worse, on the very eve of the Conference the first Anglo-Catholic Congress met in London and was popularly interpreted as being an effort to intimidate the Conference, whatever may have been the intentions of those who originated the idea. No wonder, then, that we find Gore writing to Davidson : 'I hope that Divine Providence intends the Church of England to exist over the next year or two without a schism which would separate off the Catholic section, but I dread the Lambeth Conference and its consequences.'[9]

Despite these fears, the Conference was an outstanding success. Bishop Weston caused no trouble, and even contributed much to smoothening out the difficulties which confronted the assembly.

A new and striking plan was adopted on the question of reunion when the famous 'Appeal to all Christian People' was formulated. In the years since 1920 this Appeal has become a classic among reunion documents. Every word of it has been subjected to the closest scrutiny, and contradictory interpretations have been found for almost every clause in it. Criticisms of it have come from the Catholic side, from the Eastern Orthodox, and from the Free Churches, and it has become the basis of many of the reunion schemes which it helped to bring into being.

Our criticisms here must be brief. The strength of the Appeal lies mainly in its loftiness of tone, in the high ideal of a united church which it proposes, and in the obvious sincerity of its call to reunion. Yet on closer examination we find that from beginning to end it is evasive. While it admits that faith and baptism are alone required for membership of Christ's church, it refuses to define what that church is, and a very hazy paragraph ends with the words : 'This is what we mean by the Catholic Church.' An examination of the preceding sentences leaves one in complete doubt as to what the bishops mean by the Catholic Church. The later parts of the Appeal are equally equivocal, especially the admission that the Conference does not call in question the 'spiritual reality of the ministries of those Communions which do not possess the Episcopate.' Finally, the offer to accept from other churches a 'form of commission or recognition' of the Anglican ministry has been interpreted in so many different senses that it is impossible to attach any real meaning to it.

The great difficulty, however, arising from the Appeal is the form in which it restated the Lambeth Quadrilateral. Originally the Quadrilateral was a suggested four-point basis of unity, put forward in the American Episcopal Church in 1886 and accepted with slight modifications by the Lambeth Conference of 1888 as 'a basis on which approach may be by God's blessing made towards Home Reunion.' The text put forward in 1888 is as follows :—

> (a) The Holy Scriptures of the Old and New Testaments, as 'containing all things necessary to salvation,' and as being the rule and the ultimate standard of faith.

(b)   The Apostles' Creed, as the Baptismal Symbol; and the Nicene Creed, as the sufficient statement of the Christian faith.

(c)   The two Sacraments ordained by Christ Himself— Baptism and the Supper of the Lord — ministered with unfailing use of Christ's words of institution, and of the elements ordained by Him.

(d)   The Historic Episcopate, locally adapted in the methods of its administration to the varying needs of the nations and peoples called of God into the unity of His Church.

By the year 1920 the term 'Historic episcopate' had already become a stumbling-block in conferences with the Free Churches, and the bishops at Lambeth realized that to put forward an explicit demand for the acceptance of the episcopate by non-episcopal churches would be to condemn the Appeal from the beginning. The Quadrilateral therefore had to be re-shaped. The first two paragraphs were combined into one, various minor changes appear in the phrasing, and the 'Historic Episcopate' disappears, to be replaced by the vague 'A ministry acknowledged by every part of the Church as possessing not only the inward call of the spirit, but also the commission of Christ and the authority of the whole body.'

In our treatment of the ministry later we shall have to discuss the implications of this change in the Quadrilateral. Here we must confine ourselves to the question whether the Quadrilateral in either of its forms is a sufficient basis for the reunion of the church. Different views exist among Anglicans as to its adequacy. Thus Fr. Hebert considers it a perfect outline of a reunion scheme and takes it as the basis of his own exposition of the church.([10]) A. S. Duncan Jones believes that while the earlier form was a dry and legal statement, the 1920 Quadrilateral was 'something more persuasive.'([11]) We must rather agree with J. J. Willis who points out that the Quadrilateral leaves all the fundamental questions unanswered.([12]) Firstly, it does not tell us what the church is now or what it will be when reunited, and it assumes that the unity of the church is a human, man-made thing. Further, in the four points which it puts forward, it leaves an open question what interpretation is to be attached to each. Thus the first paragraph, while stating clearly enough the Anglican teaching on scripture as the rule of faith, does not mention its relation to the magisterium or to tradition.   The second article leaves completely open the question of the Creeds' authority and interpretation, and no modernist would refuse to accept it as it stands.   The statement on the Sacraments would be rejected by many Anglo-Catholics to-day, though in its favour it might be said that it does not explicitly condemn a belief in seven sacraments.   Both in this paragraph and in the paragraph devoted to the ministry, the changes introduced by the 1920 Conference are obviously an effort to make the Quadrilateral more comprehensive and therefore more acceptable to those outside the Church of England. It is scarcely necessary to point out that as a basis for reunion between the Anglican Communion and the Catholic Church both forms of the Quadrilateral are entirely unsatisfactory unless they be interpreted in such a way as to deprive the words of their normal meaning.   Like the Thirty-nine Articles, the Quadrilateral is a Protestant document, and only the most evasive interpretation will bring it into line with Catholic teaching.

The Lambeth Appeal was everywhere acclaimed as a magnificent triumph. 'Not only were the lions in the path overcome,' writes Dr. Bell, 'but something new and creative had been done, and a great blow struck for the Reunion of Christendom.'([13])   A copy of the Appeal was sent to the Pope, and the 1930 Conference is glad to note that a courteous reply was received, but both the length and tenor of the acknowledgment make it quite clear that the Pope was not impressed.([14])

The theology of reunion as presented by the Appeal is very important because it was accepted later as the basis for negotiations in many of the reunion conferences in which the Church of England took part.   This was due mainly to the fact that the chairman of the Anglican delegation at most of these conferences was Dr. A. C. Headlam of Gloucester, whose 'Bampton Lectures' of 1920 are so very close to the principles of the Appeal, and who was a prominent member of the Committee on Unity which formed it.   The Appeal gave a new impetus to reunion and presented a challenge to the separated churches to examine their position in relation to the idea of a universal church.   In this way at least it did some good, as it helped to take some of the sects from their narrow isolation and assisted them to realize in some way the notion of a church which transcended all limits of class and race — the idea of the church as 'catholic.'

'Catholicity' in reunion documents is a term difficult to paraphrase. It implies belief in the doctrines and practices of the undivided church, and more especially of the united church that will one day exist. It is a relative term, and its embodiment is to be found in a greater or less degree in all communions. It might often be paraphrased by the term 'pre-reformation,' as opposed to Protestantism, which in Anglican theology means simply 'pro-reformation.' 'The use of the word "catholic",' says Swete, 'must be vindicated for all churches that retain the great Sacraments, the doctrine of the Catholic Creeds, and the succession of the historical episcopate.'([15]) Catholicity for reunionists involves, too, continuity with the pre-reformation church, though the reformation, *in so far as it cleared away abuses,* is not rejected. At the same time, Anglo-Catholics believe that the aim of the whole Catholic movement must be to get away more and more from the doctrinal innovations of the Reformers, and to make the Church of England more 'Catholic' by the reintroduction of doctrines and rites which were abandoned as Romanism in the sixteenth century.

The continued refusal of the Catholic Church to take part in reunion conferences is naturally a cause of grave dissatisfaction to those who are promoting the movement. Catholicity, they hope, will be one of the outstanding properties of the future church, and here is a church admittedly catholic already, refusing to have anything to do with reunion. Two alternatives present themselves. The first is to accept the note of catholicity as proposed by the church of Rome and to accept the Pope as the centre and cause of that catholicity. The other alternative is to set up an independent test of catholicity which, without denying the catholicity of Rome, will express what the reunion idea of catholicity means. Thus is born 'non-Roman catholicity.'

Non-Roman catholicity, we are told, is that type of catholicity which has been developed outside the church of Rome. It is pointed out that the Church of England never abandoned its use of the title 'Catholic' Church, and always claimed to be part of it while refusing to be subject to papal jurisdiction. The name

'Anglo-Catholic' is then the natural title for a member of the Church of England who professes 'non-Roman catholicity' — he is catholic as much as a Roman Catholic, but simply belongs to a different obedience. Here again we see the recurrence of those fundamental Anglican ideas about membership, nationality and comprehensiveness which we have examined earlier. They all play their part in the defence of Anglo-Catholicism.

A further refinement of the idea of non-Roman catholicity is that form developed mainly in the important volume of essays entitled *Northern Catholicism*. It is an effort to introduce a sub-division into 'non-Roman catholicity,' the resulting species being Orthodox Catholicity and Northern Catholicity. It is clear that Orthodox Catholicity is a unit, a homogeneous whole. The effort to show that Northern Catholicism is a distinct and unified type of catholicism has, however, not been successful, and has not been generally accepted even by Anglican writers. It appears perhaps for the first time in Dean Inge, who bases his thesis on the racial superiority of the northern nations, and tries to show that the 'Teutonic Christianity' which they are developing is superior to that produced by Graeco-Roman civilization. 'It will certainly,' he says, 'be a new type of Christianity, neither Latin nor Greek, but corresponding to the national character of the English, German, and Dutch peoples. It will, we may presume, be strongly ethical, and marked with that blend of strenuous practicality and high idealism which belongs to our national character.'([16]) Dr. Williams would claim further that the groups involved are united not merely geographically but ethnologically and intellectually as well, and he would include in addittion the peoples of Scandinavia, and would exclude the peoples of South Germany. ([17])

The theory of 'Northern Catholicism,' distinct and unified, cannot be defended. It is based on the mythical superiority of the 'Nordic' race, and the selection of countries to which it applies is quite arbitrary. National pride and imagination too play their part in its defence, as for instance when we are told that the 'essential religious genius of the Northern peoples, where it finds unfettered expression, is of a mystical and soaring quality, appropriate to dwellers amidst the less genial aspects of Nature and beneath "grey and weeping skies".'([18]) There is to-day no bond uniting German Lutherans, Church of England adherents, Dutch Old Catholics and Scandinavian Protestants. If it be objected that only the High Church Movement in these countries are meant, then we must ask what has the climate, as well as ethnological and intellectual unity, to do with the question.

The wider concept of 'non-Roman catholicity' is no less indefensible. It is but an empty name covering the acceptance of Catholic dogma along with a denial of the papal prerogatives, and it has no defence against the argument that catholicity is guaranteed only by the supremacy and infallibility of the Pope. To refuse to accept the Pope is to refuse to accept catholicity, for the one is the measure of the other. 'As to non-Roman Catholicism', writes Père Congar, 'to be perfectly frank, we believe that there is no such thing : . . . if by Catholicity we mean the universality of unity, it cannot exist without some ecclesiastical standard of unity. And as to that we do not merely believe that it might exist ; we know that it does exist. And it is Roman.'[19]

Since catholicity as a property of the church has become popular in the reunion movement, and since it is at the same time difficult to predicate in any real sense of the non-Roman churches, a number of efforts have been made to change fundamentally the connotation of the word and then to vindicate it for these churches. Thus Goudge defines catholicity as 'to care passionately for reunion,' and as a result of this definition he comes to the very satisfactory conclusion that the Church of England is fully catholic while the church of Rome is not catholic at all ! [20] Jenkins on the other hand would identify catholicity with acceptance of the principle of 'Reformation by the Word of God,' and in this sense he is able to claim that only the Free Churches are truly catholic.[21] With regard to these usages of the terms catholic and catholicity, we can only say that they are an abuse of language and tend to create theological confusion.[21a]

In their quest for catholicity the churches seeking reunion face grave difficulties in the matter of dogma. As if to allay our fears, Anglican writers frequently warn us that dogma is all-important in the solution of reunion problems, and they tell us that a reunion without dogma will not last. Thus the 1948 Lambeth Conference says that in all reunion schemes the theological issues should be faced at the very beginning, and Noble sees in the renewed interest in theology in the Anglican Communion one of the most hopeful signs of reunion.([22])   'Where dogmas don't matter,' writes V. A. Demant, 'there are merely collisions in a fog.'([23])

Despite these protestations, an examination of any of the reunion documents will show that they have really only one basis—compromise. Where possible, the parties agree on a formula which is wide enough to include both opinions, but where the two views are obviously contradictory, so that no formula however vague could cover both, each side is ready to sacrifice at least a little of what it believes, and always with the excuse that this is done in the cause of Christian charity.   Fr. Hebert says truly that 'there is a tendency to a light-hearted acceptance of schemes for reunion, while we mumur that Christian love counts for more than orthodoxy.'([24])   This habit of paring away dogma in order to arrive at a compromise has in its turn caused the resurrection of an old heresy which is now central in the theology of reunion, though very little mentioned — the theory of Fundamentalism.

The system known as Fundamentalism probably owes its origin to the French Calvinist Peter Jurieu, who claimed that the doctrines of the Christian faith can be divided into fundamental and non-fundamental, the former alone being necessary and obligatory.([25])   The modern version of the theory would apply this principle to the problem of reunion, and would take as its motto the phrase *in necessariis unitas, in dubiis libertas.*   For reunion, it is said, all that is necessary is that the churches agree on the fundamental, necessary dogmas of Christianity, and then they can afford to differ about all other matters.   The Lambeth Quadrilateral is an implicit acceptance of the principle of fundamentalism, and most reunion hopes are built on the same foundation.

Illustrations of the acceptance of some form of fundamentalism could be given from almost every Anglican writer, though the words 'fundamental' and 'non-fundamental' are not commonly used, and though the terminology is different in the different writters, the teaching is basically the same in all, with merely a difference of emphasis.

We have already discussed two of the main elements in Bishop Gore's teaching — his Liberalism and his anti-modernism.   The third element, without which the other two would be incomplete, is Fundamentalism, which he propounded and defended in the most explicit terms. He firmly believed that there were certain fundamental dogmas of Christianity which no one could deny while claiming to remain a Christian. He thus condemned the Modernists for denying the central dogmas of the faith, and on the other hand he complained that the church of Rome was putting non-fundamental dogmas (like the Immaculate Conception) on the same level as the Resurrection and the Virgin-Birth. When he put forward this teaching in his paper at Malines, the divergence from Catholic teaching appeared so absolute that the Conversations were virtually terminated.([26])

It may seem surprising that conferences like the Malines Conversations should be terminated almost immediately after the statement of fundamentalism by a member of the Anglican delegation. Yet if we realise what fundamentalism means, it will not appear strange that this result should have followed Gore's paper, for fundamentalism implies a denial of Catholic teaching on the nature of the act of faith and of the authority of the church. Gore's paper apparently had the support of the other members of the Anglican delegation, and it brought to the fore the real difference between the Catholic Church and the Church of England.

While we can admit the distinction of fundamental and non-fundamental in a wide sense in the Catholic Church, the distinction does not exist in relation to dogmas of faith. Pius XI is almost certainly referring to Gore's exposition of fundamentalism when he writes : 'it is never lawful to employ in connection with articles of faith the distinction invented by some between "fundamental" and "non-fundamental" articles, the former to be accepted by all, the latter being left to the free acceptance of the faithful.'([27])   Besides the obvious theological difficulty against it from the nature of faith, fundamentalism as a system stands condemned by the fact that no two writers have ever been able to agree as to what are fundamental doctrines and what are not. 'The assumption often made,' writes Fr. Hebert, 'that there is general agreement on the central doctrines of the Christian Faith, and that it is only the problems of the Church and the Ministry that are in dispute, is superficial.'([28])   In other words, the theory is plausible enough in itself, but it cannot be reduced to practice. Gore himself would find it difficult to name even one or two 'fundamental' articles which would not be contradicted by some party in the Church of England, and reunion efforts during the last fifty years have shown that among the different churches there is no body of doctrine common to all. What one sect considers to be a fundamental doctrine is rejected as false by another.

In a booklet which gained some notoriety when it first appeared, a Catholic priest under the pseudonym 'Father Jerome' suggested that the Catholic Church should receive back Anglicans on a basis similar to that of fundamentalism. He argued that since Anglicans left the church in the sixteenth century, they should be received back into the church now with an obligation to believe only articles of faith that were held explicitly in the sixteenth century. This line of argument is open to the objection which we have raised against fundamentalism, namely, that it rejects the authority of the church as a teacher of divine revelation, and it accepts the possibility of members of the Catholic Church refusing to believe part of the *depositum fidei*. In reply to a similar appeal for the acceptance of the distinction between fundamental and non-fundamental doctrines, Bishop Beck wrote that 'to ask a Catholic to consider such a suggestion would be similar to asking a teacher of arithmetic to make "concessions" in the results of the multiplication tables for the sake of pupils who got into a muddle over their sums.'[29]

In the present chapter we have been able to give the theological principles behind reunion schemes only in a general way and with little illustration. In the following chapters we shall go on to examine a number of schemes of reunion in which we shall see these principles being put into practice.

NOTES TO CHAPTER IV

(1) *Mortalium Animos*, in Messenger, *Rome and Reunion,* p. 85.

(2) R. A. Knox, *The Belief of Catholics,* p. 232. For some further reasons for the growth of interest in reunion, see Henry St. John, O.P., *Essays in Christian Unity,* Chapter 1.

(3) J. E. L. Newbigin, *The Reunion of the Church,* p. 14.

(4) J. W. C. Wand, in Mackenzie, *Union of Christendom,* ii. 407.

(5) Gore, *Dominant Ideas and Corrective Principles,* p. 35.

(6) H. B. Swete, *The Holy Catholic Church,* p. 83.

(7) Mackenzie, *The Confusion of the Churches,* p. 174.

(8) On the Kikuyu controversy, see infra, Chapter VIII.

(9) Bell, *Randall Davidson,* p. 1004.

(10) A. G. Hebert, *The Form of the Church,* p. 13 ff.

(11) A. S. Duncan Jones, in Williams and Harris, *Northern Catholicism,* p. 468.

(12) J. J. Willis, in *Towards a United Church,* p. 21.

(13) Bell, *Randall Davidson,* p. 1014.

(14) Text in Bell, *Documents,* i, 30. The Pope's letter runs to just over five lines and is non-committal.

(15) Swete, op. cit., p. 41.

(16) W. R. Inge, *The Church and the Age,* pp 55 ff.

(17) N. P. Williams, in Williams and Harris, *Northern Catholicism,* p. ix.

(18) Williams, op. cit., p. xi.

(19) M. J. Congar, O.P., *Divided Christendom,* p. 197. The whole treatment of catholicity it outstanding, and see p. 94 where he defines the church's catholicity as 'the dynamic universality of her unity.'

(20) H. J. Goudge, *The Church of England and Reunion,* p. 236.

(21) D. J. Jenkins, *The Nature of Catholicity,* passim.

(21a) In fairness, it should be mentioned that one occasionally meets with sincere appeals for theological precision, e.g., E. L. Mascall, *Lambeth 1958 and Christian Unity,* p. 18.

(22) W. J. Noble, in *Towards a United Church,* p. 10.

(23) V. A. Demant, in Mackenzie, *Union of Christendom,* i. 57.

(24) Hebert, op. cit., p. 104.

(25) See A. Tanquerey, article 'Articles Fondamentaux,' in *D.T.C.,* col. 2027 ff.

(26) On this very significant paper, see infra, Chapter VII.

(27) *Mortalium Animos*, in Messenger, *Rome and Reunion,* p. 84. The whole encyclical seems to have Anglican theology especially in mind.

(28) Hebert, op. cit., p. 73.

(29) G. A. Beck, in *The Times,* November 15, 1949.

CHAPTER V

THE CHURCH OF ENGLAND AND THE ORTHODOX CHURCHES

The relations between the Church of England and the Eastern Orthodox Churches are one of the most interesting developments of the reunion movement. Despite a keen desire by sixteenth century reformers in England for recognition by the Orthodox, and despite the efforts of the reforming Patriarch Cyril Lucar in the following century to maintain friendly relations with the Church of England, nothing had been achieved up to the beginning of the present century. The 1908 Lambeth Conference could report no more than friendly contacts through the Anglican bishopric at Jerusalem, and Dean Inge, writing in 1912, could see no point in 'associating with the State-Church of a semi-barbarous autocracy, sunk in intellectual torpor and gross superstition.' [1] A real start, however, was made in 1921, when the patriarch of Constantinople issued an encyclical letter suggesting means whereby the various churches could become more friendly and try to understand one another better. After the publication of this letter matters developed quickly, and in 1922 the patriarch on behalf of the Orthodox Church of Constantinople declared Anglican Orders to be valid. To understand the situation, however, we must first examine briefly the Eastern Orthodox teaching on the nature of the church and sacraments.

The Eastern churches are a number of 'autocephalous' or independent bodies, making up between them the one Orthodox or True Church. According to Orthodox teaching, all who do not belong to the Orthodox Church are heretics, and they are not in any way members of the true church. The Orthodox is then exclusively the One True Church, and so absolute is this exclusiveness that there are no sacraments and no grace in any other church. Even the sacraments of the Catholic Church are regarded as invalid, and some would hold that if the Roman Church were to be converted to Orthodoxy even the Pope would have to be rebaptized. However, by means of the principle of Economy (Oikonomia), the Orthodox may accept as valid the sacraments already received by those who are converted to Orthodoxy, but there can never be a general validation by the Orthodox of the sacraments of other communions, for these communions are not the church and cannot therefore have valid sacraments. It is difficult to find a parallel in Western theology for the principle of Economy, and Eastern theologians have rejected any that have been put forward. I would suggest that the Pauline privilege in marriage embodies fundamentally the same principle — Economy and the Pauline privilege are both a change of sacramental status in favour of a convert. It is a very important principle in Orthodox sacramental theology, as it affects the whole question of the validity of Anglican orders.

The attitude of the Orthodox to the reunion movement is a strange one. Holding the doctrine of exclusiveness even in a more absolute form than the Catholic Church, they are yet willing to take part in conferences of the Ecumenical Movement. That they are really committed to the doctrine of exclusiveness is quite clear from the statements made by their delegation at the Lausanne Conference in 1927. When the reports on 'The Nature of the Church' and on the 'Common Confession of the Faith of the Church' had been drawn up, the delegation declared : 'The drafting of these two latter was carried out on a basis of compromise between what in our understanding are conflicting ideas and meanings, in order to arrive at external agreement in the letter alone,' and after insisting on notes, exceptions, and other special declarations of their own point of view, they finally stated that with the exception of the first report, 'they were not to be regarded as having concurred in receiving any of the other Reports.' The present writer's own view is that their main interest in the Ecumenical Movement is a vague hope of thereby making converts to Orthodoxy.

In 1931 the Joint Doctrinal Commission appointed by the Archbishop of Canterbury and by the Patriarch of Constantinople met to discuss points of agreement and disagreement between the two communions. Nine of the Orthodox Churches were represented, and the Anglican delegation was led by Dr. Headlam of Gloucester. It was noteworthy that before the discussion began at all, the chairman of the Orthodox delegation insisted on making a statement to the effect that Sacramental Communion would be allowed by the Orthodox only as the last step of reunion when complete dogmatic agreement had been established. This seemed to be intended as a reminder to Anglicans that they were negotiating for return to the One True Church and that they should not entertain any hopes of easy intercommunion with it.

Of the various questions discussed during the Conference, the subject of Tradition as a source of authority interests us most. The doctrine of the Orthodox as put forward by the Metropolitan of Thyateira was that 'the teachings which were necessary to salvation were drawn from two sources of Revelation — Scripture and Tradition.'([2]) The Anglican delegation on the other hand insisted on the sufficiency of scripture as set forth in Article VI of the Thirty-nine Articles. In drawing up the report, a compromise was resorted to. Apart from a vague common statement subscribed to by all, the conference had to be satisfied with a plain juxtaposition of contradictory beliefs, under the two headings : 'the representatives of the Anglican Church would say . . .' and for the Easterns : 'the representatives of the Eastern Orthodox Church would say . . . .'

On the subject of the Sacraments, the same fundamental difference is clear in the teaching of the two communions, and we have again the two contradictory opinions simply placed side by side unreconciled. On the Trinity, the Anglicans were strangely liberal and rejected both the term Filioque and the doctrine underlying it. In the common statement on Tradition we find the following :—

> 'We agree that by Holy Tradition we mean the truths which came down from Our Lord and the Apostles through the Fathers, which are confessed unanimously and continuously in the Undivided Church, and are taught by the Church under the guidance of the Holy Spirit.'

Obviously this statement can be interpreted in a Catholic sense, and was meant to be so interpreted by the Orthodox delegation, but if we ask what the Anglicans meant by the church in this context the difficulties begin to appear. In the same declaration the Anglicans accepted the sufficiency of Scripture 'as completed, explained, interpreted, and understood in the Holy Tradition.' As one Anglican comment points out, everything depends on what was meant by 'completed,' and in any case it is quite inconsistent to say that the Scriptures are sufficient by themselves and at the same time to say that they are sufficient only when completed by Tradition. Anglican theology on the nature and function of Tradition will have to change radically if there is to be reunion with the East, for at Lausanne the Orthodox delegation declared : 'We Orthodox cannot conceive a united Church in which some of its members would hold that there is only one source of divine revelation, namely, Holy Scripture alone.'([3])

The question of the validity of Anglican orders and the nature of the ministry in general is another insurmountable obstacle to the reunion of the Church of England with the Eastern Orthodox Churches. The attitude of the Orthodox to Anglican orders down through the centuries was based on the principle which we have already explained, namely, that there are no valid sacraments outside the Orthodox church, and this attitude was unchanged right up to the year 1920. After that year, however, a number of declarations were made by some the the Eastern churches, and many Anglican writers to-day boast of the fact that the Church of Rome is almost the only communion which positively asserts the invalidity of Anglican orders. They point to the list of statements by the Orthodox churches asserting that Anglican orders are valid, and at least some of the documents seem to be quite clear and explicit in their acceptance. What then, we may ask, has happened to Orthodox theological principles in the last forty years ?

In the first place, not all the Orthodox churches have made declarations on the validity of Anglican orders. The main churches which have so far accepted them are Constantinople (1922), Jerusalem and Cyprus (1923), Alexandria (1930) and Rumania (1936), along with a partial recognition by the Greek Orthodox in 1939. The position of the Orthodox Church of Russia is peculiar and will need separate treatment, but even apart from the Russian church it is obvious that only a part of the Orthodox communion has accepted Anglican orders, and the only great Orthodox Church to do so is the patriarchate of Constantinople, or, as it is called, the Ecumenical patriarchate.

The circumstances in which the patriarchate of Constantinople accepted Anglican orders were very strange and illustrate well the Anglican principle of 'facing both ways' which he have already noted. When it became known in England that the Ecumenical patriarch was considering making a statement on Anglican orders, a Declaration of Faith was drawn up by Anglo-Catholics and forwarded to him. This document was signed by Bishop Gore and other prominent High Churchmen, and ultimately received the signatures of 3715 clergymen of the Church of England. (4) Dr. A. C. Headlam (later bishop of Gloucester) strongly objected to the Declaration as being entirely incompatible with the official formularies of the Church of England and especially with the agreement which had been drawn up with the Free Churches in the very same month. (5) Despite strong protests the Declaration was presented to the patriarch as containing the official teaching of the Church of England.

We have already noted the idea of the church as set forth in this declaration of Anglican faith. (6) It accepted the Orthodox teaching that the church is composed of a number of churches which are 'autokephalos' and 'autodioketos' (self-administered), and went on to declare that the Church of England officially accepts seven sacraments and apostolic succession. The purpose of the priesthood, it said, was 'that we who are priests should (a) preach and teach the word of God ; (b) offer the unbloody sacrifice of the Eucharist for both the living and the departed ; (c) sacramentally absolve sinners who repent and confess their sins ; and (d) otherwise minister to the flock of Christ according to the ancient faith and practice of the Universal Church.' The real objective presence of Christ in the Eucharist was admitted, and the consecrated Species declared to be the object of adoration by the faithful. The Thirty-nine Articles were brushed aside as a document of secondary importance concerned with local controversies of the sixteenth century.

It must be admitted that this Declaration of Faith was but a travesty of the official teaching of the Church of England. If it had been presented as the teaching of the Anglo-Catholic party it would have been fair enough, but to send it to the patriarch as being the official teaching of the whole Church of England was deliberately to mislead the authorities in Constantinople. However, it obtained the desired effect, and on July 28, 1922, the Ecumenical Patriarch in a letter to the Archbishop of Canterbury accepted Anglican orders as valid. We are told that Davidson received the recognition with courtesy, but made every effort to show that the acceptance of Anglican orders by other churches did not in any way affect their validity. Yet we may well believe that this recognition by an Orthodox church after Anglican orders had been rejected by the Catholic Church was a source of real satisfaction — another proof that Rome had been wrong.

Nevertheless, the declaration by the patriarchate of Constantinople was not without important qualifications. It stated firstly that before this acceptance of Anglican orders could become an 'Ecumenical Act' and therefore binding, it must be accepted by all the other Orthodox churches. The patriarch knew quite well that because of the differences, political and otherwise, among the various Orthodox churches, there was little possibility of getting them all to accept the declaration. The second qualification was equally important, and said that despite the fact that Anglican orders are in future to be accepted as valid, intercommunion or mutual administration of the sacraments must not take place. It would seem that once the Anglican priesthood was accepted as a real priesthood the Orthodox should have no objection to Anglican priests ministering to Orthodox church-members separated from their own priests, but this is explicitly forbidden. This is one of the most important factors to be taken into account in the evaluation of the Orthodox acceptance of Anglican orders.

The next three recognitions of Anglican orders may be taken together. The first two were in the year 1923 and came from the patriarch of Jerusalem and the church of Cyprus ; then in 1930 the patriarch of Alexandria informed Archbishop Lang that he too accepted the validity of Anglican orders. It has been suggested, and with great probability, that these three decisions were prompted by a desire to please the British authorities who had political control of the territory of all three churches at the time the declarations were made. Whatever may have been the real reason for this action by the three churches in question, it is

curious that the Church of England should receive confirmation
of the validity of its orders from churches which its own formularies declare to have erred in matters of faith — 'sicut erravit
ecclesia Hierosolymitana, Alexandrina . . . .'([7]) Finally, as a
result of a conference held in Bucarest in 1935, the Holy Synod
of the Orthodox Church of Rumania accepted Anglican orders
as valid in 1936. In 1940 conferences were held with representatives of the Serbian Church in Belgrade, again under the chair-
manship of Dr. Headlam, but nothing definite resulted. Conferences with the Bulgarian Church resulted in the acceptance
of Anglican orders 'in principle', but the war broke off these
latter contacts.

Earlier in this chapter we noted the Orthodox sacramental
principle of Economy, and posed the question of its relation to
these statements of the validity of Anglican orders. The reports
of the Lambeth Conferences make no reference to the over-ruling
principle of Economy and accept the declarations at their face
value, namely, as declaring valid without qualification the orders
possessed by Anglican bishops and ministers. Many Anglican
writers do likewise, and we are given the impression that the
Eastern recognition was a simple, unqualified acceptance. Even
a brief examination of Orthodox theology, however, shows that
this was not the case, and that the declarations were subject to
the over-riding principle of Economy. The position would then
be that while Anglican orders are invalid (because outside the
Orthodox church) they may be recognised as valid by Economy
if individual Anglicans are converted to Orthodoxy, and this
principle of Economy would really be a sort of legal fiction accepting as valid what had been really and objectively null and void.

This solution is in full accordance with Orthodox principles
as we have already expounded them, and it also agrees with the
general Orthodox expectation of the future conversion of all
other communions to Orthodoxy. Some few Anglican theologians
admit that this is the real meaning of the recognitions. Mackenzie
says that they mean that Anglican orders have all the conditions
necessary for validity except the absolutely vital one of being
within the True Church,([8]) and Goudge admits that 'it means
little more than that, if the Anglican Church became . . . .
an "Orthodox" Church, our priests would not need to be re-

ordained.' (9)   The number of such forthright admissions is exceedingly small, but if further evidence were required as to the real meaning of the Orthodox declarations, we have two explicit statements on the point, one from the Orthodox Church of Greece and the other from the Orthodox Conference held in Moscow in 1948.

British friendship for the Greek nation is traditional, and hence it was surprising that the Orthodox Church of Greece did not follow the line taken by the Ecumenical patriarch in 1922 in relation to Anglican orders. It was not until September 21, 1939, that a statement on the subject was issued by the Holy Synod, and this statement was by no means complimentary to Anglicans, despite the fact that it was issued mainly with a view to soliciting British aid in the war, which had broken out a few weeks previously. The Resolution passed was a follows :

> The Orthodox Church recognizes as valid without qualific-
> ation only those sacraments which she has herself
> administered, but that nevertheless the Church . . .
> recognizes by Economy the Ordination of those who come
> over to Orthodoxy. (10)

The statement is clear on the principles of Orthodox theology, and may be set forth in three propositions :   (i) no sacraments outside the Orthodox Church are valid ;   (ii) yet in the case of converts to Orthodoxy these same sacraments may be accepted ; (iii) this recognition will be given by means of the principle of Economy. The declaration could not be more explicit, and it sums up perfectly the Orthodox attitude to Anglican orders. The con- clusion to be drawn is therefore that Anglican orders are invalid in the eyes of the Orthodox Churches, and the sacraments of Anglican bishops and ministers are equally null and void. It is small consolation to Anglicans to know that they will not be reordained if they become converts to Orthodoxy.

The attitude of the Russian Orthodox Church towards the Church of England is difficult to determine, since the political situation must always be taken into account. The Lambeth Conference of 1930 expressed regret that no Russian delegation was able to attend its meetings, and it is quite likely that a delegation would have been present but for the persecution which broke out in the Russian Church in 1929. The 1948 Conference welcomed the re-establishment of relations between the two churches after the war, and stated that a *modus vivendi* appeared to have been reached with the Soviet State authoritories concerning the position of the church. It was very noticeable, however, that the Eastern churches were not well represented at the 1948 Conference, which in that respect compared very poorly with the previous one. Again we cannot know how far the question of politics entered, but it does not seem to have been a coincidence that at the same time as the Lambeth Conference was being held in London, a Conference of the Orthodox Auto-cephalous Churches was being held in Moscow, and this seems to be the real reason why no high dignitaries of the Eastern churches appeared at Lambeth in 1948.([11])

The document on Anglican orders issued by the Moscow Con-ference of 1948 confirms our suspicion that political considerations occupy an important position in the determination of the relations between the Orthodox and Anglican communions. Allowing for this, however, the whole theological teaching which it contains is faithful in the smallest detail to the principles of Orthodox theology. The document is such an important one that we give here a short summary of it, with quotation of some of the more important points :

i) Anglican doctrine as contained in the Thirty-nine Articles differs sharply from the teaching of the Orthodox churches, and before any decision can be reached on the question of Anglican orders, the Church of England must be ready to agree to the Orthodox teaching on the Sacra-ments. If some autocephalous churches have already recognised Anglican orders, *we are informed that these recognitions were conditional.*' (Italics ours).

ii) This agreement of the teaching of the Church of England with Orthodox doctrine must be drawn up in an authoritative conference and presented to the Orthodox churches. 'In this connection we express our desire that the Anglican Church will change its doctrine from the dogmatic, canonical and ecclesiological point of view.'

iii) Finally the Conference decreed : 'That the contem-porary Anglican hierarchy may receive recognition of the grace of its Orders from the Orthodox Church if, between the Orthodox and Anglican Churches, first of all will be established a formal expression . . . of Unity of Faith and Confession. After instituting this desire for Unity, the recognition of validity of Anglican Orders can be realized under the principle of Economia.'[12]

In view of what we have said already, this resolution of the Moscow Conference needs little comment. It contains the usual Orthodox teaching on the church, the sacraments, and the principle of Economy, and, on theological grounds at least, no Anglican theologian could quarrel with it. What makes it so important, however, is that it has said with an explicitness not apparent in the earlier statements that Anglican orders are in the eyes of the Orthodox Churches null and void. The 1948 Lambeth Conference said that the main cause of delay in the full recognition by the Orthodox as a whole of Anglican orders was the impossibility of holding a pro-Synod, which alone could decide the question authoritatively and in such a manner as to be binding on all the autocephalous churches. The Conference did not seem to be aware that a pro-Synod or at least something very similar to one was at that very moment being held in Moscow and was drawing up a declaration on the subject of Anglican orders very different from what the Anglican bishops expected. This statement of the Moscow Conference is a *reductio ad absurdum* of the claim that the Orthodox Churches have recognized the validity of Anglican orders. In effect, the Orthodox churches have rejected Anglican orders on even more fundamental grounds than the Catholic Church has done.

In view of this latest development and in view of the political situation, it is very difficult to see what the future holds for Anglo-Orthodox relations. Many of the Orthodox churches are entirely under Russian domination, and the freedom allowed to them at present may be only apparent. It is certain, however, that because of the sufferings which they have undergone in the past few years they must be considered heroic in the defence of the Christian faith as they see it. Their contribution to the movement for Christian unity is no less valuable because of the difficulties, both political and theological, that hinder its development.

* * * * * *

As a contrast to the Anglican failure to achieve intercommunion with the Eastern Orthodox, it may not be out of place to append here a short account of the agreement reached between the Church of England and the Old Catholic Churches. As is well known, the Old Catholic churches were formed by the union of Jansenist supporters who fled into Holland in 1723 and Catholics who refused to accept the Vatican Council's definition of papal infallibility in 1870. The two elements came together in the Union of Utrecht in 1889, and their profession of faith, called the Declaration of Utrecht, is mainly a rejection of papal infallibility, the Immaculate Conception and the anti-Jansenist pronouncements. Otherwise they hold practically the whole of Catholic belief and they practise most of Catholic liturgy.

We can see immediately that it is quite natural for the Church of England to have strong leanings towards the Old Catholic churches, for their existence is a living protest against the papal claims and a perfect example of that 'non-Roman catholicism' which Anglicans admire so much. Meetings were held at Bonn in 1874 and 1875 at which Anglicans, Eastern Orthodox and Old Catholics met, and some measure of agreement was reached, but nothing further was done until the present century. The Lambeth report of 1878 is however worth quoting as a typical example of the nineteenth century Anglican attitude to the Catholic Church, for, speaking of the Old Catholics, it says : 'The fact that a solemn protest is raised in so many Churches and Christian communities throughout the world against the usurpations of the See of Rome, and against the novel doctrines promulgated by its authority, is a subject for thankfulness to Almighty God.' The Conference of 1878 prayed for the removal of the many barriers which separated the two communions.

Despite this friendly attitude, relations became somewhat estranged between the two communions over the Bishop Mathew case. Mathew was a Catholic priest who first joined the Church of England and later, in 1908, got himself consecrated bishop by the Old Catholics with a view to setting up a branch of the Old Catholic church in England. He believed that by so doing he would win over many Catholics and Anglicans, and in anticipation of large-scale conversions he consecrated a number of bishops and ordained many priests in England. After a strong protest by the Lambeth Conference of 1908, the Old Catholics realized the anomaly of his position and broke off relations with him. The Lambeth Conference of 1920 thanked them for their action and declared : 'We regret that on a review of all the facts we are unable to regard the so-called Old Catholic Church in Great Britain (under the late Bishop Mathew and his successors), and its extensions overseas, as a properly constituted Church, or to recognize the orders of its ministers.' The report presented by the committee which discussed this question, while making every effort to disprove the claim of the 'Old Catholic Church in Great Britain' to be a real church, is obviously afraid to deal with the fundamental question of what constitutes a church. On the other hand it did not wish to appear to be casting any doubt on the validity of Old Catholic ordinations in general, so it suggested the safe compromise of conditional reordination for the ministers of Bishop Mathew's church. It is suggested that this decision means that the Church of England has accepted the position that ordinations by a bishop without the authority of the church are invalid. Once the Mathew affair was settled, relations became friendly again, and in June 1925 the Archbishop of Utrecht formally recognized the validity of Anglican orders without quali- fication. The conference of Old Catholic bishops held at Berne in September of the same year endorsed the Archbishop's action.

In 1931 a joint doctrinal commission of the Church of Eng- land and the Old Catholics met at Bonn.([13]) All of the questions asked by the Old Catholics in the course of the conference showed their deep suspicions of what they called 'Protestanism' in the Church of England. The answers supplied by Dr. Headlam, chairman of the Anglican delegation, were admirably evasive, although the many interruptions of an Evangelical (Mr. Graham- Brown) on the Anglican side must have caused even Dr. Headlam some difficulty. After a long discussion an agreement was drawn up, based on a document prepared by Mr. Graham-Brown. The text is as follows :

1. Each communion recognizes the catholicity of the other and maintains its own.

2. Each communion agrees to admit members of the other communion to participate in the sacraments.

3. Intercommunion does not require from either communion the acceptance of all doctrinal opinion, sacramental devotion, or liturgical practice characteristic of the other, but implies that each believes the other to hold all the essentials of the Christian faith.

This agreement is clearly a compromise reached between two churches which have scarcely a single doctrine in common, and its brevity is explained only by the fact that the churches could not find any real measure of agreement. It is difficult to know what is meant by 'catholicity' in the first paragraph, and the number of sacraments is left quite open in the second, since the Evangelical delegate on the Anglican side refused to subscribe to any phrase which might imply that there are more than two. It is curious, too, that the terms of agreement between two churches claiming to be 'catholic' should have been dictated by an Evangelical, and it shows once more the strength of Protestantism in the Church of England to-day. The agreement was ratified by the Old Catholics in Vienna in September 1931, and by both Convocations of the Church of England in the following January.

It seems strange that the efforts of the Church of England to reach agreement with two non-Lutheran churches should result in complete intercommunion with one and complete disagreement with the other. The explanation is to be found partly in the exclusiveness of the Orthodox churches which demand dogmatic agreement as a preliminary to intercommunion, and partly in the Old Catholics' belief that like the Church of England their own church is destined to be a 'bridge-church' between East and West. It is important to note, however, that in both cases the idea of a universal church as expounded by Anglican theologians is no more than a loose federation of independent national churches. There is no thought at all of corporate reunion under a central authority.

NOTES TO CHAPTER V

(1)   W. R. Inge, *The Church and The Age*, p. 62.

(2)   *Lambeth Occasional Reports*, (Orthodox), p. 67.

(3)   Bell, *Documents*, ii. 27.

(4)   Text in Bell, *Documents*, i, 90 ff.

(5)   Bell, *Randall Davidson*, p. 1105; the agreement with the
      Free Churches is entitled 'Church Unity, May 1922.' For
      the text, see Bell, *Documents*, i. 143.

(6)   See above, Chapter II.

(7)   Article XIX of the Thirty-nine Articles.

(8)   Mackenzie, *The Confusion of the Churches*, p. 238.

(9)   H. L. Goudge, *The Church of England and Reunion*, p. 65.

(10) Bell, *Documents*, iii. 50.

(11) See W. Zylinski, "The Russian Church in Soviet Politics,"
      in *The Eastern Quarterly*, vol. iii, no. 2 (April 1950) p. 20 :
      'The ambitious aim to establish a Third Rome in Moscow
      as the Orthodox centre of the whole world has persisted
      in the minds of the leaders of the Church and rulers of the
      state for centuries.' For an account of the Moscow Con-
      ference, see pp. 23-5. (art. cit.)

(12) The text of the declaration in so far as it relates to
      Anglican orders is given by J. L. Monks, S. J., "The
      Orthodox Churches on Anglican Orders," in *Theological
      Studies*, vol. x, no. I, (March 1949) pp. 65-6.

(13) Text of report and minutes in *Lambeth Occasional Reports*,
      (Old Catholics), p. 7 ff.

CHAPTER VI

THE MINISTRY AND THE FREE CHURCHES

The Lutheran idea of the church universal as primarily an invisible society had immediate repercussions on the doctrine of the ministry. Since the Christian attains justification by Christ's merits imputed to him, he needs no intermediary in his relations with God and he is his own priest. The doctrine of the 'priesthood of all believers' involves further that if ministers are required to preach the gospel and rouse up justifying faith, their authority will come not from a special charism conferred in succession from the apostles, but from appointment by the flock to whom they will minister. This difference between the Catholic and the Lutheran concept of the ministry is sufficiently expressed by saying that the Catholic ministry is 'from above' and the Lutheran 'from below.'

Article XXIII of the Thirty-nine Articles gives us very little information on the teaching of the Church of England on the subject of the ministry. It says merely that in order to minister in the church a man must be 'called' and 'sent' to do this work by those in the church who have the power to 'call' and to 'send.' It is the result of an earlier compromise between Lutherans and Anglicans who were able to agree on the necessity for a 'call,' but 'any further agreement about the nature of the authority that could confer ordination, whether episcopal or presbyterian, could only be attained by vagueness.'(¹) The very vagueness of the Article, however, rather suggests a Lutheran meaning, and the definite Lutheran tendencies of the Ordinal imply at least that the Lutheran idea of the ministry was not entirely foreign to the Church of England in the sixteenth century.

The Free Churches in England to-day are the doctrinal heirs of Lutheran teaching on the church and the ministry. Holding as a fundamental tenet the doctrine of an invisible church, they

teach that the Church becomes visible in local independent congregations — whence the names Independents and Congregationalists. Besides the sects which came in from the Continent, there
were many schisms from the Church of England, the first three
occurring before the end of the sixteenth century, namely in
1568, 1572 and 1586. To-day these are banded together in a
loose type of organization called the 'Free Church Federal Council'
which, while uniting them for common action in relation to the
outside world, allows each congregation absolute freedom in
matters of doctrine and liturgy. They recognize no condition of
membership of the church beyond the confession that 'Jesus is
Lord'; while using creeds they refuse to accept them as a pre-
requisite of membership, and they take up the same attitude
towards baptism. They invite all Christians indiscriminately to
participate in their Eucharist, of which they believe all laymen
(and women) to be the minister. 'A Church is constituted,'
writes a leading Congregationalist, 'not by its possession of a
particular form of Church government, but by the presence in
it of Christ, Who alone is the Church's head'.[2]

The Church of England has ever been solicitous for reunion
with the groups which have broken away from her, but it is only
in the present century that serious efforts at reunion have been
undertaken. In 1916 some meetings were held between delegations appointed by the Archbishops of Canterbury and York
and by the Free Churches, but the two Interim Reports which
were issued show that the commission never succeeded in getting
down to the real differences which separated the two sides.[3]
A sentence, however, occurs in the second report which was later
to become a classic in reunion conferences, for the two sides
agreed that 'acceptance of the fact of Episcopacy and not any
theory as to its character should be all that is asked for.'[4]
It is significant that the distinction was at this early stage being
formulated between the 'fact of episcopacy' and the 'theory' behind
it. The Free Churches had already found the weakness in the
Anglican armour.

Of the many replies received in acknowledgment of the Lambeth
Appeal of 1920, that of the Free Churches is by far the most
extensive and the most critical.[5] It subjected the whole of the
Appeal to a very thorough examination, and strongly asserted the

position of the Free Churches. It pointed out that the Appeal passed lightly over the most fundamental element in reunion, namely, agreement about 'vital principles regarding the Church, and, still more, regarding the Gospel,' adding that the essentials of the church are to be found in the Gospel and not in organiz·ation. On the vague attitude taken up by the Appeal, the reply commented: 'As we read the Lambeth Appeal, it logically implies that our communions, like episcopal communions, are already parts of the visible Church of Christ. But, if this be the correct interpretation of the Appeal, it should be made clear that it is so.'

. In the years following the Appeal, many conferences were held beween the Church of England and the Free Churches on the subject of reunion. In a Joint Report issued in 1922, we find the usual refusal to define exactly the nature of the church and the relation of the visible to the invisible in it : 'This one Church consists of all those who have been, or are being, redeemed by and in Christ, whether in this world or in the world beyond our sight, but it has its expression in this world in a visible form. Yet the Church, as invisible and as visible, is, by virtue of its one life in Christ, one.'[6] It is difficult in this definition to see whether the visible or invisible church is being discussed, and the last sentence says plainly that the source of the church's unity is its allegiance to the invisible Christ. Later when we find a distinction made between the notes of the church as applied to the ideal church and as applied to the actual church, we are forced to conclude that the report is a compromise from which each side may take the meaning that suits it.

During the course of these meetings the Free Churches adopted a practice which Anglicans must have considered most unfair. Having appointed a delegation with power to discuss matters of reunion with the Church of England, and having received the re·ports signed by both parties, the Assembly of the Free Churches proceeded more than once by way of 'Resolution' or 'Memorandum' to a long condemnation of practically everything in the reports. In one such Resolution, the Assembly, while rejecting most of the Joint Commission's report, welcomed the statements which declared the 'essentially spiritual character of the Church of Christ,' and regarded this as meaning that no true believer is out·

side the church. This shows that whatever the report originally meant, the Free Churches would insist on interpreting it to mean an invisible church. The whole Resolution is a defence of that Lutheran doctrine.

Undaunted by set-backs such as this, the conferences continued their work. The Free Churches apparently could not understand the Anglican refusal of intercommunion while they themselves were ready to welcome all believers in Christ to their sacraments and all 'ministers of the word' to their pulpits. In a Memorandom presented by their Federal Council in September 1924, (7) the suggestion was made that the conference should not be indefinitely prolonged, and the Council stated that efforts at reunion between the two bodies would lack reality until Anglicans permit full intercommunion between them. It is curious to see the Free Churches seeking intercommunion with Anglicans and being refused, and at the same time to see Anglicans seeking intercommunion with the East and being openly rebuffed. In the following year the refusal of the Free Churches to accept anything even approaching conditional reordination caused the suspension of the meetings altogether.

After the 1930 Lambeth Conference joint meetings were again resumed, and in 1938 the delegates drew up the *Outline of a Reunion Scheme* which went into great detail about the future organization of what it called 'the united Church of England', even suggesting that during the period of 'growing together' there should be a plural episcopate in each diocese in England. Baptism was insisted on as a condition for membership of the future church, though it was stipulated that some sort of limited membership might later be found for the Quakers. This scheme of reunion was accepted by both Convocations of the Church of England, but once again the Free Churches repudiated the action of their delegates and rejected the proposals. In a long memorandum they pointed out that very many members of the Free Churches consider reunion neither necessary, desirable, nor practicable, and they refused to accept baptism as a pre-requisite for membership. Despite this clear statement of the Free Churches' belief, the Archbishop of Canterbury again appointed a commission to discuss the question of reunion with them, and since 1942 the organisation known as the British Council of Churches has been in existence, its purpose being to bring the two sides together for discussion of matters of common interest. In the year 1960, in deference to the wishes of its Congregationalist members, the Free Church Federal Council decided to abandon its plan of setting up a commission to study differences between its member-churches.

The real difficulty between the Church of England and the Free Churches is, of course, the question of the ministry. The Free Churches believe, and Anglicans do not deny, that non-episcopally ordained ministries have been abundantly blessed by the Holy Spirit, and the Free Church position is that because of their spiritual efficacy these ministries must be recognized as valid in any scheme of reunion. A reordination or re-commissioning of any kind is therefore entirely unacceptable to them, and thus a deadlock is reached between the two sides. In every re-union scheme this difficulty has appeared at some stage, and it is now generally recognized to be the main obstacle to all forms of reunion. Dr. Kirk rightly points out that the doctrine of the ministry involves ideas on the nature of the church and hence on the nature of God, [8] and says that as plans and conferences have progressed it has become obvious that the real crux is whether the ministry is 'from above' or 'from below.' Goudge shows that the ministry cannot be discussed apart from the church, [9] and the Bishop of Manchester, speaking at the Lausanne Conference, warned the delegates that agreement to differ on the subject of the ministry would ensure disruption of any scheme of reunion formulated on such a basis. [10] Yet, as we shall see, not a single reunion scheme has faced up to the difficulty raised by the doctrine of the ministry, and in each case the problem has been solved either by ambiguous language or by compromise.

The fundamental principles on the subject of the ministry accepted generally in Anglican theology are mainly two. There is first the insistence that episcopacy, (whether it be of the *esse* or only of the *bene esse* of the church as a whole) is the only method of church government which is lawful for the Church of England to-day. The second principle is no less important, and states that no Anglican has a right to reject the spiritual efficacy of other ministries, even if they are not episcopally ordained. These two principles can be traced back to the sixteenth century, to

the attitude of the English reformers to the non-episcopally
ordained ministries of their day, and they are fundamental in
contemporary Anglican theology. The 1908 Lambeth Conference
stated the Anglican position very clearly :

> Anglican Churchmen must contend for a valid ministry
> as they understand it and regard themselves as absolutely
> bound to stipulate for this for themselves and for any
> Communion of which they are members. But it is no
> part of their duty, and therefore not their desire, to go
> further and pronounce negatively upon the value in God's
> sight of the ministry in other Communions.

The same two principles were enunciated by Archbishop Davidson in his pamphlet closing the Kikuyu controversy, in which he
maintained that while Anglicans must maintain the three-fold
apostolic ministry in their own communion, they are not bound to
hold that others who follow a different system of government are
thereby outside the church.([11])

These two principles work fairly well while the churches are
separate, but they clash once an effort is made at reunion. Will
the episcopal church recognize the validity of the orders of the
non-episcopal church? The Lambeth Quadrilateral had tried to
solve the difficulty by demanding as a condition of reunion the
acceptance of the 'historic episcopate.' What exactly was meant
by the phrase when the Quadrilateral was first drawn up we
cannot know, but very soon the Free Churches had attached to it
a meaning which turned it into an empty catchword. As early
as 1916, as we have noted, a distinction was drawn between the
'fact' of episcopacy and particular theories as to its meaning ; the
Free Churches claimed that they were being asked to accept the
fact of episcopacy and refused to be bound to any particular
interpretation of that fact. Thus at a conference in 1922 it was
agreed that 'the acceptance of Episcopal Ordination for the future
would not imply the acceptance of any particular theory as to its
origin or character.' The Lambeth Conferences did not reject the
distinction, and insisted merely that the Historic Episcopate com-
prised both an office and functions, a point which no Congregationalist would deny.

The practical result of this distinction is that to-day the acceptance of the historic episcopate by the Free Churches — if ever

they accept it — means merely the assumption of a new name with no real change in status. Thus Wedel welcomes the phrase 'historic episcopate' as containing none of the serious implications of the earlier term 'apostolic succession,'([12]) and a Baptist writer, speaking of the possibility of his church accepting the episcopate, says that if it merely means a new plan for administration, then 'a change of name would hardly raise difficulties.'([13]) It it of little use to insist on the word 'historic' as part of the phrase, for if it implies apostolic succession the Free Churches will have none of it, and in any other sense it can add very little to the meaning.

That the acceptance of the episcopate merely as a kind of honorary title by the Free Churches would be of little assistance to the cause of reunion does not seem to have been felt by Anglican writers generally, and the first serious protest against the abuse of the term 'historic episcopate' was the excellent volume of essays edited by Bishop Kirk of Oxford under the title *The Apostolic Ministry.* Deploring the fact that in reunion schemes the phrase means absolutely nothing, Dr. Kirk points out that it is the apostolic power represented by the bishop's office that non-Anglicans must accept with a view to reunion,([14]) and Dom Dix asks the all-important question : 'What *could* be meant by "the historic episcopate" apart from one particular "theory" of its nature and origin ?'([15]) He concludes that if we are logical we must admit that 'apart from that "particular theory of its origin and nature" there is simply no such thing as the "historic episcopate" at all.'([16]) The phrase has, however, become such a part of the theology of reunion now that it is extremely unlikely that the notion of it will be clarified. It has, as Dom Dix admits, a certain diplomatic value, and that is something which must at all costs be preserved, no matter what the theologians say to the contrary.

The Lambeth Quadrilateral as reshaped by the Conference of 1920 in the Appeal to all Christian People did not demand the historic episcopate as a basis for reunion. It suggested instead 'a ministry acknowledged by every part of the Church as possessing not only the inward call of the Spirit, but also the commission of Christ and the authority of the whole body'. The change seemed at the time a most important one, as it appeared to involve at least a possibility of Free Church ministries being recognized by the

Church of England. Other paragraphs of the Appeal seemed to admit the full validity of non-episcopally ordained ministries, and the question of reunion turned for a moment from the acceptance of the episcopate by the Free Churches to the recognition of Free Church orders by the Church of England.

It is generally admitted by Anglicans that in the sixteenth and seventeenth centuries sometimes, if not frequently, men who had not been episcopally ordained were allowed to minister in the Church of England, and Anglicans normally received Communion from ministers of Reform Churches on the continent. Anglican theologians traditionally refused to 'unchurch' or declare invalid such ministries, though as to their positive validity there is silence. The 1920 Appeal is, however, strangely near a positive assertion of validity when it says : 'It is not that we call in question for a moment the spiritual reality of the ministries of those Communions which do not possess the Episcopate'. These words imply clearly enough that the Free Church ministries are real ministries capable of doing what the Church of England ministry claims to do, and Dr. Cadoux seems to be interpreting the words in their natural meaning when claims that they recognize the Free Churches as 'possessing a true and valid Christian ministry'.(17)   In a Memorandum prepared by the Anglican representatives at a conference with the Free Churches in 1923, the language of the 1920 Appeal was made even more definite : 'Such Free Church ministries we find it impossible to regard as "invalid," that is, as null and void, or as effecting none of the purposes for which the ministry has been Divinely ordained in the Church of Christ.'([18]) This statement is certainly very close to a declaration of positive validity. Dr. Headlam in his 1920 Bampton Lectures had already asserted the validity of the orders possessed by the Free Church ministries.([19])   It would seem, then, that the Church of England was ready to abandon the demand for the acceptance of the historic episcopate and was ready to receive non-episcopal ministries on equal terms with its own.

The hopes of the Free Churches for the acceptance of their orders as valid were doomed to disappointment. The Lambeth Appeal in a moment of over-generosity had somehow implied the validity of these ministries, but in calmer times it was realized that it had gone too far. 'We were glad at first,' wrote Jeremy

Taylor in the seventeenth century, 'of abettors against the errors of the Roman church ; we found these men zealous in it . . . and we were willing to make them recompense by endeavouring to justify their ordinations, not thinking what would follow upon ourselves'.([20]) The parallel with the Appeal is perfect. Here again the consequences appeared too great, and a process of withdrawal began. The historic episcopate made its appearance again, and Anglicans spoke of the Lambeth Quadrilateral as if the 1920 conference had not changed it essentially by omitting all mention of the episcopate. In the semi-official booklet *The Doctrine of the Church* we are told that Anglican theologians differ on the subject of the validity of non-episcopal ministries,([21]) and the 1938 Report on doctrine notes a 'divergence of opinion' among the members of the Commission on this subject.([22])

An effort had to be made, however, to justify the statements made in the Appeal, and after 1920 we find everywhere a distinction drawn between the 'spiritual reality' or 'effectiveness' of a ministry and its 'validity.' The Appeal, we are told, was not dealing with the question of validity at all, and when it accepted the 'spiritual reality' of non-episcopal ministries it meant just that, and had no thought of the question of validity. We find, too, long discussions everywhere of the meaning of 'valid' as distinct from 'efficacious,' and the 1930 Lambeth Conference, as if anxious to show that it was not withdrawing anything said in the Appeal, stated : 'we emphatically declare that we do not call in question the spiritual reality of the ministries now exercised in non-episcopal communions'. It carefully avoided, however, any use of the word 'valid', and the implications of the statement are therefore clear. The bishops were refusing officially to say that Free Church ministries were positively valid. No Anglican theologian has, however, succeeded in finding a basis for the distinction between 'validity' and spiritual reality'.

The Anglican attitude to Free Church ministries becomes clearer when we examine the question of reordination. It is the traditional Anglican teaching that non-episcopally ordained ministers should be reordained before being allowed to minister in the Church of England, but the 1920 Appeal asked them to receive merely 'a commission through episcopal ordination.' The reply of the Free Churches not unfairly pointed out that the phrase was ambiguous and asked that the point should be clarified, insisting at the same time that they would never accept anything implying reordination.   The bishops suggested instead of ordination a solemn form of 'authorization,' or alternatively ordination *sub conditione*.   The Free Churches insisted that there were implications in both proposals — namely, that they were being asked to accept the priesthood and admit the invalidity of their own orders — and negotiations were suspended. If the bishops were sincere in their offer of a form of 'authorization' not implying ordination, they would seem to be accepting the position that what the Free Churches need is not the power of orders but the power of jurisdiction.   This failure to distinguish clearly between the two types of power is frequently met with in schemes of reunion.

The real source of Anglican hesitation in relation to Free Church ministries is ultimately due to the fact that the Church of England has never made up its mind whether or not it believes episcopacy to be a part of the divinely constituted form of the church, or, to use the current phraseology, it cannot decide whether episcopacy is of the *esse* or merely of the *bene esse* of the church. If episcopacy is of the *esse* of the church, then non-episcopal ministries are not ministries of the Christian Church, and reunion with them will involve reordination. On the other hand, if it is admitted that the office of bishop is something of human origin, we can foresee circumstances in which it may be dispensed with ;   yet, the argument runs, even though it is a human institution, it was necessary for unity in the past and will be necessary for the attainment of unity in the future.   Thus both views arrive at the same conclusion about the necessity of episcopal ordination in the future church, though they begin from diametrically opposed views as to its origin.

In the present century the clearest denial of the New Testament origin of the episcopate came from Dr. Headlam in his famous Bampton Lectures of 1920.   He taught explicitly that neither episcopacy nor any other form of church government could base itself on the New Testament. 'It seems to me clear,' he wrote, 'that not one of the rival systems of Church polity which prevail at the present day can find any direct support in the New Testament'.([23])   In suggesting a basis for the future reunion of the church, he claimed that the New Testament laid down directions not for any particular form of ministry but merely intended that a properly organized ministry of some kind should exist in the church. Not a few Anglican theologians accept Headlam's view, and the 1938 doctrine report admits that it is the opinion of scholars that more than one kind of ministry can be found in the New Testament, whereupon it proceeds to reject the authority of the New Testament in the solution of the problem of the ministry. [24]

Even those Anglicans who reject the belief that episcopacy can be defended from the New Testament will not reject episcopacy altogether. They will, together with the vast majority of Anglicans to-day, say that the bishop's office is necessary for the *bene esse* of the church. They do not, however, seem to realize that this theory involves the further belief that the episcopate is of purely human origin, though they would probably be prepared to admit this conclusion if it were forced on them. Such a conclusion would of course be quite acceptable to the modernist group. 'No fair-minded man,' writes Bishop Barnes, 'could examine the contribution made by the Presbyterians to Christian civilization and assert that episcopacy, however convenient and sanctioned by long tradition, was essential in Christ's church', [25] and Rashdall says that a church which has got rid of the ministry of prophets could also get of the ministry of bishops without ceasing to be Christ's church. [26] It is another indication of the spread of modernist principles that the divine origin of the episcopate should be so widely denied in contemporary Anglican theology.

The claim is strongly advanced that the Church of England has never officially stated that episcopacy is of the *esse* of the church. The refusal to unchurch non-episcopally ordained ministries involved, it is argued, the admission that episcopacy was not of the *esse* of the whole church, and it is pointed out that the custom of reordaining such ministers did not reflect in any way on their former status, but was a lawful requirement of the national church. To-day emphasis is laid more on the usefulness of the episcopate, as if its divine origin were indefensible and as if it were now necessary to prove against the Free Churches that at least it is useful, that it is of the *bene esse* of the church. Except for a small section of Anglo-Catholics whom we shall mention presently, Anglican theologians seem to be content to vindicate for their church the utility rather than the absolute necessity of the episcopate.

To deny that episcopacy is of the *esse* of the church is another way of saying that apostolic succession is not necessary, and this seems to be the real centre of debate in the argument between the two sides.   Once apostolic succession is denied, you are left with the meaningless 'historic episcopate' of which we have spoken above, and this is all that is meant by many of the writers who hold that episcopacy is only of the *bene esse* of the church.   Thus Dr. Matthews, speaking at a reunion conference with the Church of Finland, said that he would consider belief in apostolic succession in the sense of episcopal imposition of hands to be 'sub-Christian'.([27])   He would, of course, insist nevertheless that episcopacy was of the *bene esse* of the church. Palmer believes that the continuous Christian tradition that episcopal succession was absolutely necessary must give way, in view of modern circumstances, to the teaching that it is merely the best of many possible methods.([28])   The 1938 Report with its usual appearance of thoroughness collects five arguments in favour of episcopacy as the best method of church government, and seems to admit the weakness of its case by stating that these five arguments must be taken together, for 'the argument for Episcopacy derives its strength from the convergence of many different considerations.'([29])   For Bicknell, the succession of bishops from the apostles is not part of a divinely instituted plan, but rather 'apostolic succession represents the intellectual justification of a practical necessity'.([30])   Many rejections of apostolic succession could be quoted from other contemporary Anglican theologians.

The view which we have been discussing, namely that the episcopate is not of the *esse* of the church but merely of its *bene esse,* is far removed from Catholic teaching.   The Council of Trent laid down clearly that there is in the Catholic Church by divine ordinance a hierarchy consisting of bishops, priests and ministers.   Despite the general Anglican repudiation of this definition, there are yet some Anglo-Catholics who would be prepared to accept it in the literal sense.   Thus Foster writes : 'It is impossible to insist too strongly upon this matter of

Apostolical Succession, *since the whole theory of the Catholic Church rests upon it,* and no Sacrament can be valid unless it is administered by a validly ordained ministry.'[31] Another writer puts the matter in an amusing but forceful way when he says that 'the real Anglican view is the Catholic view that even though any particular set of Bishops may not seem to be of the *bene esse of* the Church, they are nevertheless of the *esse* of it.'[32]

In view of the admitted Anglican friendship for non-episcopal churches after the reformation, it would be difficult to prove that this is the traditional Anglican view, though it is claimed that a scientific study of the great Anglican theologians will lead to that conclusion. Fr. Hebert outlines what he considers to be the six strongest arguments against episcopacy being of the *esse* of the church, and he demolishes them all just as a Catholic theologian might do.[33] Finally, the whole thesis of the great work *The Apostolic Ministry* is that, whatever may have happened during the second half of the first century, there can be no doubt that the ministry of the apostles was transmitted to their successors and that from them the power and authority of the apostles has passed into the Christian church.[34]

We have mentioned these writers individually in order to show that a small section of the Church of England to-day strongly holds something approaching the Catholic teaching on the subject of episcopacy and apostolic succession. It must be insisted, however, that this group is only a small minority and cannot claim to represent the whole church. Officially, then, there is a 'divergence of opinion' on the subject in the Church of England. The early Anglican theologians can be quoted on both sides, as is shown by the volumes of extracts from their writings published by both parties in the controversy. Hodgson, in the semi-official booklet already quoted, says that the Church of England neither asks nor answers the question whether apostolic faith or apostolic ordination constitutes the ministry.[35] This refusal to give a definite decision on the position of the episcopate was brought out clearly when in a discussion at the 1930 Lambeth Conference the pointed question was put by the Orthodox : 'Does the Anglican church agree that Holy Orders is a *mysterion,* and that, in its succession, it is a link with the Apostles ?' By way of reply, the patriarch was referred to the Prayer Book, the Thirty-nine

Articles and the Preface to the Ordinal, but no effort was made to answer the question which he had asked. This policy of refusing to take a definite stand on the question of the episcopate was taken a stage further by the Lambeth Conference of 1948, when the Committee on the Unity of the Church boldly faced the question whether episcopacy is of the *esse* or merely of the *bene esse* of the church and replied that both views must be accepted and 'room left for varying interpretations of the fact of episcopacy'. As regards the tensions set up by the acceptance of two such contradictory beliefs in one church, the committee declared in a typical Anglican apologia :

> We acknowledge them to be part of the will of God for us, since we believe that it is only through a comprehen-siveness which makes it possible to hold together in the Anglican Communion understandings of truth which are held in separation in other Churches, that the Anglican Communion is able to reach out in different directions, and so to fulfil its special vocation of one of God's instruments for the restoration of the visible unity of His whole Church.

Comprehensiveness and the Bridge-Church idea are again called upon to justify what appears to the outsider to be a patent con-tradiction.

These theological difficulties about the nature of the episcopate have, as we have seen, been very apparent in the relations of the Church of England with the Free Churches, and they are appear-ing in practically all the schemes for reunion. Not unnaturally it was suggested that there should be some way of achieving unity in practice while leaving the theological dispute aside for the present. The Free Churches had positively rejected even con-ditional reordination, and something less unpalatable had to be found. Here an Anglican principle which we have discussed earlier was brought into play. This principle laid down that all churches are at present in schism, and the conclusion drawn in relation to the ministry is that the orders possessed by any given church are only partial orders, and to get a proper Christian ministry for the future united church, every denomination must give to every other denomination the partial grace and authority of orders that it possesses. This theory, known as Supplemental

Ordination, seemed to be the solution of many reunion problems, as it avoided the one-sidedness of conditional reordination while at the same time guaranteeing that each ministry would get from the others whatever it lacked. The theory was clearly outlined by Dr. Headlam in a speech at the Lausanne Conference, in which he claimed that 'because the Church is divided therefore all Orders are irregular and no succession is perfect. The unity of two branches of the Christian Church must come by each giving what it can to the other in the ordination of its clergy.' ([36]) While we cannot admit with Bishop Neill that this is the view held by the vast majority of Anglican churchmen, ([37]) it seems to be the underlying principle of many of the suggestions put forward for unification of the ministry.

The theory of Supplemental Ordination is open to many objections even from the point of view of Anglican theology. Thus Mascall insists that the whole scheme is pointless since ordination comes not from the imperfect and partial manifestations of the church that exists on earth but from what he calls the 'archetypal' or ideal church. ([38]) It is obvious, too, that if the theory is taken to its logical conclusion the number of supple-mental ordinations must be almost infinite because of the vast number of sects into which, according to this view, the church has disintegrated. The Lambeth Conference of 1948, having accepted a statement on the relative strength of the arguments for and against the theory, refused to identify itself with either view and contented itself with stating both, 'side by side and unreconciled'.

We cannot over-estimate the importance of the ministry for the whole question of reunion. The Church of England by refusing to decide the question of the position of the episcopate is living up to its reputation of being the Bridge-Church between Catholic-ism and Protestantism, but it is at the same time refusing to answer some of the most fundamental questions in all theology. It is refusing to say whether the ministry is 'from above' or 'from below,' refusing to say whether it believes in a visible or in an invisible church, refusing to say whether the Church of England wants to be Catholic or Lutheran. As we have pointed out already, it cannot logically be both.

Many practical difficulties are causing Anglican theologians to take up one side or the other in the discussion on the nature of the ministry. We have seen that it was the problem of reunion that first raised the question, and reunion is still the main cause of the continuance of the discussion. However, of late years a new and at first sight an unimportant question has come to the fore, and may in the near future cause one of those periodic crises which have been a feature of the life of the Church of England in the present century. We refer to the question of the Ministry of Women, or the possibility of Deaconesses being ordained to the priesthood in the Anglican Communion.

The Oxford Movement was mainly responsible for the introduction of religious orders for women in the Church of England, and very soon it became common for some of these sisterhoods to call their members Deaconesses. Their first official recognition came from the Lambeth Conference of 1897 which hailed with thankfulness the revival of this ancient office, and gradually a form of ordination or admission to the office of deaconess became common, though the actual rite was left to the bishop of each diocese. Bishop Gore was quite enthusiastic about the amount of work they could do, and he insisted that of all the regulations laid down by St. Paul about the position of women in the church only one involved a matter of principle — the limitation of the priesthood to men. Little did he realize that very soon it would be claimed that all the apostle's directions on this subject were on an equal footing, that all were particular instructions given for particular times, and that all must now be swept aside because of changed circumstances.

By the time the 1920 Lambeth Conference came to be held, the position of women in the church had become a very important subject and a special committee was set up to consider it. The Report suggests a form for the ordination of deaconesses and sets forth a detailed list of their duties. The committee offered the opinion that the ordination of a deaconess conferred on her the character of Holy Orders, and at the same time tried to stop any efforts that might be made to get the priesthood for deaconesses by saying : 'We believe that for Women the Order of Deaconess is the one and only Order of the Ministry which has the stamp of Apostolic approval : and for Women it is the one and only

Order which we can recommmend that our Branch of the Catholic Church should recognize and use.' This statement was endorsed by the whole conference, though a proposal to allow deaconesses to preach was passed by 117 votes to 81, thus showing that a majority of the bishops were not quite satisfied with the office of deaconess as it had been accepted, and that they were willing to give it at least part of the privileges and obligations of the priesthood.

The 1930 Conference brought matters a stage further. The Committee reported that it had received from many quarters an urgent plea for the admission of women to the priesthood, but it refused to encourage such petitioners in any way, and the whole conference repeated the 1920 Resolution that the only order for women was that of Deaconess. It laid down further details about the functions to be assigned to Deaconesses, as if hoping that a widening of their powers might make them satisfied with their office.

The first official proposal that women should be ordained to the priesthood came from the diocese of South China through the General Synod of the Chinese bishops to the Lambeth Conference of 1948. It suggested that in the Church of China deaconesses should be ordained to the priesthood provided they possessed certain qualifications. The Chinese bishops who were on the committee dealing with the proposal argued that, since Anglican tradition and order were based on the autonomy of national churches, this 'liberty to experiment' should be granted to the church in China. Wisely and bravely the committee decided that the proposal must be rejected. It recalled the Lambeth resolution of 1930 on the subject and insisted that 'Anglican tradition and order have certainly not hitherto recognized or contemplated the ordination of any woman to the priesthood.' The whole conference was still more definite and said that such an experiment would gravely affect the internal and external relations of the Anglican Communion. A loop-hole was, however, left by the statement that the time has not come for the further formal consideration of the subject, but the conference showed clearly its attitude to the ordination of women when it said that a serious obstacle had been set up against the possibility of relations with the Church of Denmark because of the recent ordination of three women to the priesthood in that Church.

The bishops of the Anglican Communion have taken up a definite attitude to the ordination of women to the priesthood, and no doubt the vast majority of their own subjects will agree with their decision. There is, nevertheless, a strong element in some of the churches of the Anglican Communion which accepts the Lutheran conception of the ministry and will strive to vindicate the full ministerial powers of the church for women. When the General Synod of the Church of Ireland decided to permit women to enter church posts in 1949, a member declared that the measure might lead eventually to women entering the ministry. If that happened, he said, many people like himself would be 'constrained to sever our connections with the Church.'

The question has once again taken a practical turn with the ordination of three women to the priesthood in Sweden on Palm Sunday, 1960. The decision had been taken two years previously and had split the Swedish church into opposing camps. However, the 1960 ordinations, taking place on the same day in three distinct places, are evidence of a deliberate movement towards a priesthood of women in a church which has had close ties with the Church of England. Only time will tell what success will be achieved by the boycott of these Ordinatae organized within the Swedish church; the repercussions in the Church of England will perhaps be of even greater interest. Many Anglicans, especially the more conservative type, would certainly not tolerate a priesthood of women in any form. We may well expect a crisis over this particular problem in the years to come.

NOTES TO CHAPTER VI

(1) E. J. Bicknell, *A Theological Introduction to the Thirty-nine Articles,* p. 404, where the author says that 'the history of the Articles accounts for its vagueness'. See also Messenger, *The Reformation, the Mass, and the Priesthood,* ii. 294 ff.

(2) R. K. Orchard, in *Towards a United Church,* pp. 179-180.

(3) Text of both reports in Gore, *Dominant Ideas,* pp. 38-51.

(4) Ibid., p. 49.

(5) Text in Bell, *Documents,* i. 120-142.

(6) Ibid., i. 147.

(7) Ibid., ii. 73.

(8) Kirk, *The Apostolic Ministry,* p. 32.

(9) H. L. Goudge, *The Church of England and Reunion,* p. 24.

(10) H. N. Bate (Ed.), *Faith and Order, Lausanne, 1927,* p. 136.

(11) Bell, *Randall Davidson,* p. 705.

(12) T. O. Wedel, *The Coming Great Church,* p. 144.

(13) R. Ashworth, in Mackenzie, *Union of Christendom,* ii. 535.

(14) Kirk, *The Apostolic Ministry,* p. 46, 52. On the relative unimportance of names in this discussion, see Arthur H. Ryan, *The Church of Christ,* p. 95.

(15) Dix, in *The Apostolic Ministry,* p. 297.

(16) Ibid., p. 298.

(17) Cadoux, *Catholicism and Christianity,* p. 650

(18) Bell, *Documents,* i. 158.

(19) A. C. Headlam, *The Doctrine of the Church and Christian Reunion,* p. ix.

(20) Quoted in N. Sykes, *The Church of England and Non-Episcopal Churches in the Sixteenth and Seventeenth Centuries,* p. 4.

(21) L. Hodgson, *The Doctrine of the Church as held and taught in the Church of England,* p. 26.

(22) *Doctrine in the Church of England,* p. 134.

(23) Headlam, op. cit., p. 88.

(24) *Doctrine in the Church of England,* p. 117. This view is also defended by W. K. L. Clarke, in Jenkins and Mackenzie, *Episcopacy, Ancient and Modern,* p. 1 ff.

(25) E. W. Barnes, *Should Such A Faith Offend ?,* p. 262.

(26) H. Rashdall, *Christus in Ecclesia,* p. 116.

(27) *Lambeth Occasional Reports,* (Finland), p. 166. **Dr.** Matthews did not of course mention that this 'sub-Christian' belief was widely accepted in the High Church party of the church he was representing.

(28) E. J. Palmer, *South India,* p. 18.

(29) *Doctrine in the Church of England,* pp. 122-3.

(30) E. J. Bicknell, *A Theological Introduction to the Thirty-nine Articles,* p. 423. He has already drawn a distinction between episcopacy and apostolic succession, p. 416.

(31) A. E. M. Foster, *Anglo-Catholicism,* p. 78 (Italics ours).

(32) S. C. Carpenter, in Martin, *Towards Reunion,* p. 50

(33) A. G. Hebert, *The Form of the Church,* p. 110 ff.

(34) See especially in *The Apostolic Ministry* : Farrer, p. 150 ff; Dix, p. 228 ff., p. 292 ff.

(35) Hodgson, op. cit., p. 25.

(36) H. N. Bate, *Faith and Order, Lausanne,* 1927, p. 333.

(37) S. C. Neill, in *Towards a United Church,* p. 136.

(38) E. L. Mascall, *Christ, the Christian, and the Church,* p. 123, note.

CHAPTER VII

ANGLICANISM AND ROME

Since the separation of the Church of England from the Catholic world in the sixteenth century various efforts at rapprochement were made without, however, attaining any lasting success. It is clear that the early reformers believed that to be in communion with the Roman Church meant being outside the Catholic church, and this attitude survived in Anglican thought almost to the beginning of the present century. It is reflected in some of the resolutions of the earlier Lambeth Conferences ; the Conference of 1878, for instance, warned the faithful that the act done by the pope in the Vatican Council was 'an invasion of the attributes of the Lord Jesus Christ'. The next Conference declared that it was useless even to consider the question of reunion with Rome, and the Conference of 1897 voted sympathy for 'the brave and earnest men . . . who have been driven to free themselves from the burden of unlawful terms of Communion imposed by the Church of Rome'. In the previous year 'Apostolicae Curae' had declared Anglican orders invalid, and relations between the Catholic Church and the Church of England seemed to be as bad as they could possibly be.

In the Conference of 1908 there is a completely new attitude towards the Catholic Church which it is difficult to explain. The bishops found many changes for the better in the Latin Church and desired to place on record their conviction that no plans of reunion can be satisfactory if they forget the Latin Communion, towards which they advised an attitude of courtesy on the part of all their subjects. Despite infrequent reappearances of the 'No Popery' attitude since 1908, the Lambeth Conferences as a whole have been quite friendly, and some of them have repeated the statement, now famous, of the 1908 Conference that 'there can be no fulfilment of the Divine purpose in any scheme of reunion which does not ultimately include the great Latin Church of the West'.   This declaration at least reminds us that Anglicans have not been entirely forgetful of the possibility of reunion with the Catholic Church.

On the other hand, it cannot be said that the Catholic Church has been unmindful of reunion and especially of the approaches made by the Church of England.   In 1895 Leo XIII wrote the Apostolic letter 'Amantissima Voluntatis' to the English people, in which he said :   'With loving heart, we turn to you all in England, to whatever community or institution you may belong, desiring to recall you to this holy unity'.   Since then many other encyclicals on the subject of the church's unity pay special attention to the position of the Church of England and its attitude to reunion.   Pius XI set up at Amay a congregation of Monks of Unity who pray and work for the cause of reunion, and the annual Church Unity Octave has the same end in view.

Very little change has come since 1896 in the question of the validity of Anglican orders.   The bull *Apostolicae Curae* put an end to Anglo-Catholic hopes, and nothing has since occurred to suggest that the decision should be altered.   Leo XIII, writing to Cardinal Richard of Paris, declared that his judgment was final — 'perpetuo firmam, ratam, irrevocabilem' — and in relation to the question of Anglican orders was meant 'absolute judicare penitusque dirimere'.   Although the Bull received much criticism, its main thesis stands unchallenged — that Cardinal Pole was commanded by Pope Paul IV to reordain all who had been ordained during the reign of Edward VI, showing thereby that from the beginning the Catholic Church did not recognize Anglican orders.   The publication by Dr. Messenger in 1934 of the newly-discovered Ordinal of Martin Bucer showed that the Anglican Ordinal is not based on the Sarum rite but is Lutheran in origin, and gave, if such were necessary, another guarantee of the correctness of the decision of 1896.([1])   There is no likelihood of the question being re-opened.   The Catholic Church, therefore, holds quite definitely that Anglican orders are invalid, and the Church recognizes no such practice as the 'Economy' of the Easterns.   Anglican orders can be validated only by reordination, though one Anglican writer considers that in the event of corporate reunion the Catholic Church might not demand more than conditional ordination.([2])   The point is a purely theoretical one.

The problem of Anglican orders is certainly a great obstacle to the reunion of the Church of England with the Catholic Church. It is not, however, by any means the most important one, and it would probably cause very little difficulty if ever the question of corporate reunion arose. Far more serious is the centuries-old tradition of prejudice and open hostility towards the 'foreign priest', and the very word 'Rome' has in Anglican writings taken on a sinister meaning. One still finds the same charges of Mariolatry and idolatry made against Catholic worship. All this will have to be cleared away if there is to be any attempt at friendship, let alone reunion.

Most important of all, however, in the eyes of Anglican theologians, is the attitude of the Catholic Church to the question of authority. It is, they believe, the one great obstacle to reunion. Thus at a reunion conference with the churches of Latvia and Estonia, the Bishop of Derby said that before any effort could be made at reunion with the Catholic Church, 'the Roman doctrine of authority would have to be drastically revised'.([3]) This is not surprising in view of what we have said already about the Anglican doctrine of authority, which amounts to a denial of any real authority in the church. It denotes a fundamental difference between the Catholic and the Anglican conception of the nature of the church and of the powers left to it by its Divine Founder, and it will be of very little use to consider proposals for reunion which do not begin at the nature of the church.

In regard to the question of authority and other fundamental differences between the Catholic Church and the Church of England, most Anglicans seem to have the idea that Rome will change sooner or later. They do not seem to realize, however, that for the Catholic Church to change its attitude to, for example, infallibility, would be to deny its position as the church of Christ. From the Catholic point of view, either Rome is the whole Catholic Church or the Catholic Church no longer exists in the world. Yet Anglicans constantly look for, and think they find, signs of change in these matters in the Catholic Church. Thus the members of a Lambeth Committee in 1930 are not without hope that the Church of Rome may in some parts of the world change at some future date, and Dr. Wand is equally hopeful when he says that it is not true that 'Rome cannot change'.([4])

Another writer believes the Church of England to be the most suitable agent for forcing Rome to adapt herself to the rest of Christendom.([5])   These and the numerous other writers who believe that it is possible for the Catholic Church to change her doctrine where matters of faith are concerned have a very in-adequate understanding of the church's teaching.

The argument against the Roman notion of authority is, of course, directed primarily against papal supremacy and infalli-bility. We find frequently in High Church writers an admission of a primacy together with a denial of supremacy. 'It is fully admitted', writes Swete, 'that from early post-apostolic times the Roman Church enjoyed an honorary primacy among the churches of the empire',([6]) and Bishop Wood says that the primacy of the Roman church is readily acknowledged as a matter of history.([7]) Quotations to the same effect could be multiplied. The pope is accepted as patriarch of the West and as possessing a certain primacy of honour over all other bishops, even something more than a primacy of honour, yet it is felt at the same time that the only way to make the Vatican decrees of 1870 acceptable will be to explain them away. The 1938 report on doctrine says that the Church of England was right to oppose the claims of the papacy in the sixteenth century and is still bound to oppose them to-day, though the Commission is divided as to whether there should be room for any kind of papacy in the future church.([8])   The 1948 Lambeth Conference notes that there has been no abatement of the demand for submission to the papacy since 1928, when the Encyclical *Mortalium Animos* was published, and declares that there is still no possibility of its being accepted by the churches of the Anglican Communion.

The Anglican claim against the papacy is based directly on the text of the New Testament. Nowhere in the gospels, the argument runs, is anything special given to St. Peter. Some-times he receives powers from Jesus in common with the rest of the apostles ; at other times he receives power in the name of the rest and as their representative ; nowhere does he receive anything peculiar to himself. Some would reject the Petrine text in St. Matthew's gospel (xvi, 18) as an anachronism because of its use of the term ecclesia,([9]) while of those who accept the text as authentic some would refuse to accept the identification of the 'rock' with the person of Peter. Bishop Gore, with perhaps the majority of Anglicans, would accept the position that Peter is the rock on which the church is to be built, but he would say that it is Peter *as representative of the apostolic college* is meant.([10]) This interpretation owes much of its popularity to Hort,([11]) whose great authority is quoted in its favour, but it is in open contradiction to the plain words of the text which is obviously meant to give something personally to Peter and not to the others. 'It is important to bear in mind', wrote Leo XIII in *Satis Cognitum,* 'that nothing was conferred on the Apostles apart from Peter, but that several things were conferred on Peter apart from the Apostles'.([12]) Other Anglican interpretations of the text are no less unsatisfactory. Thus Farrer in *The Apostolic Ministry* says merely that the exact position occupied by St. Peter among the apostles can hardly be determined, and in relation to the great promise to Peter in St. Matthew's gospel has no other comment than that 'you cannot squeeze canon law out of poetry'.([13]) The 1938 Report takes up the strange position that the promise 'the gates of hell shall not prevail against it' means that physical death does not cut one off from the church, which is merely a revival of the only serious attack ever made on the text — that by Harnack, who tried to show that portae inferi meant physical death and that the text was therefore a promise of personal immortality to St. Peter.

The New Testament teaching on the position of St. Peter is of supreme importance for the proper understanding of the nature of the church, and so we must entirely disagree with Fr. Congar's suggestion that the Vatican Council definition of 1870 was an example of a one-sided development in the doctrine of the Catholic Church.([14]) We cannot, simply to avoid offending some Anglicans, omit from our definition of the church one of the main elements of it, and we cannot rightly find fault with a definition which identifies membership with submission to the bishop of Rome. The pope is not simply something added to the church after it was completed ; the pope is of the very essence of the church, and we are not making the church any more presentable to Anglicans if we lay aside the question of the papacy in our discussions. As Scheeben points out, by the very fact that in the pope lies the plenitude of pastoral power and that there can be no power in the church independent of his, 'the church is made truly and perfectly one, not only in its summit, but in its deepest base . . . Any other, lesser unity in the Church is unthinkable'.[15]

The Anglo-Catholic attitude to the papacy is a curious one. We have first of all the 'Romanizing' Anglo-Catholic who professes to accept all Catholic doctrine, including papal supremacy and infallibility, while remaining in the Church of England. It is not uncommon, we are told, for some Anglo-Catholic ministers to look to the Sacred Congregation of Rites for decisions in liturgical matters. It is quite impossible that such an attitude can continue long ; the unreality of the position is a guarantee that it will not survive. Less inconsistent it the position of those who accept Catholic doctrine in general but deny the papal prerogatives. This party fails to realize that the rejection of one dogma means the rejection of all, for all dogmas stand on equal footing as regards the authority which imposes them. Despite this rejection of some of the papal claims, all Anglo-Catholics would look forward to reunion with the Catholic Church as the first and greatest necessity — 'we belong to Western Christendom, and it is to our true Patriarch we must look first in any theory of reunion'.[16] The normal Anglo-Catholic ideal is a church centred at Rome and ruled by a 'constitutional' pope who would give 'direction' in matters of faith, but not binding the faithful with infallible decrees nor governing with universal jurisdiction. The present position of the Archbishop of Canterbury would perhaps come nearest to this ideal papacy.

A striking manifestation of this attitude to the papacy occurred in 1923 at the meeting of the Anglo-Catholic Congress. We have already noted the suggestion that the first Congress (in 1920) was held mainly to impress if not to intimidate the 1920 Lambeth Conference. The proceedings of the 1923 Congress show that Anglo-Catholics wished to demonstrate that reunion with Rome must never be lost sight of. Due mainly to the efforts of Bishop Weston of Zanzibar, a telegram was sent to the pope which read : 'Sixteen thousand Anglo-Catholics in Congress assembled offer respectful greetings to the Holy Father, humbly praying that the day of peace may quickly break'. The uproar caused by this expression of 'Romanism' in the Church of England was almost as great as that which followed the re-establishment of the Catholic hierarchy in 1850, but Dr. Prestige points out that there is no evidence that the telegram ever got beyond West-minster.([14]) Nevertheless that such a message should be sent to the pope is important as showing the Anglo-Catholic attitude to reunion. In 1932 the more advanced Anglo-Catholics issued a 'Centenary Manifesto' protesting against the modernist tendencies in some sections of the High Church party and urging that the real goal of Anglo-Catholicism was 'reunion with the Apostolic See of Rome'.([18])

The main contact between the Church of England and the Catholic Church in the present century has been the series of meetings known as the Malines Conversations.([19]) Lord Halifax, the Anglo-Catholic champion, undismayed by the condemnation of Anglican orders in 1896, still hoped for reunion with the Catholic Church, and suggested to Cardinal Mercier that some-thing might be done if theologians from both sides could meet and set about examining the differences between them. Cardinal Mercier agreed, and so the first 'Conversation' was held at Malines from the sixth to the eighth of December, 1921. Halifax was accompanied by Dr. Armitage Robinson (Dean of Wells) and Dr. Walter Frere, while Cardinal Mercier had with him Mgr. Van Roey and the Abbé Portal. In a Memorandum prepared for use at Malines, Lord Halifax wrote : 'The fundamental question which has to be decided in any discussion or conference held to promote the reunion of Christendom is, what constitutes the Church'. The first meeting was quite a successful one, and there was as yet no sign of fundamental disagreement, even though some of the main differences between the two sides had been touched upon, and it is noteworthy that when the Anglicans were brought face to face with the papacy as the only possible centre of church unity they did not altogether reject the idea.

At the second meeting (March 14-15, 1923), events took an unfortunate turn which was to effect the whole future of the Conversations. The Anglicans requested that, instead of dis-cussing the fundamental differences between the two sides, points of a more practical nature should be treated, and in particular the position which the Church of England would occupy in a reunited Christendom. The change of ground was an unfortunate one as it gave rise to hopes of agreement and moved the dogmatic questions into the background, while at the same time it completely antagonized Archbishop Davidson of Canterbury who was gravely alarmed at the suggestion (accepted by both parties) that the Archbishop of Canterbury should receive the pallium from the pope. Davidson suggested immediately that if the Conversations were to continue they should return to the most important question of all — the position of the papacy. When we examine Davidson's attitude to the Conversations generally, we are led to believe that he hoped that a serious discussion of the papacy would cause a breakdown ; whatever we may think of his motive, however, the advice which he gave was quite sound.

The third meeting, which was held in November 1923, was from the doctrinal point of view the most important. A controversy which had developed between Bishop Gore (Anglican) and Mgr. Batiffol (Catholic) suggested the two of them as extra theologians. Dr. Kidd also joined the Anglican side and Abbé Hemmer the Catholic side. The position of the papacy was once again taken up seriously, and a paper on 'The position of St. Peter in the primitive church' by Armitage Robinson was replied to by Batiffol. Several papers followed on the early use of the Petrine texts and other questions relating to the papacy. At the conclusion the Anglicans, while refusing to admit the universal jurisdiction of the bishop of Rome, were willing to accept what they called 'a spiritual leadership and a general solicitude for the well-being of the Church as a whole'. When pressed that this might be interpreted as a meaningless primacy of honour, they admitted a 'primacy of responsibility'. The admission was a notable one, and shows what an earnest discussion of the really difficult questions can attain.

If the third Conversation can be called the most important, the fourth was from many points of view the most unfortunate. The parties met at Malines in May 1925, and the meeting had scarcely opened when Cardinal Mercier read a paper without consulting any of his colleagues. It was entitled 'L'Église Anglicane unie non absorbée', and suggested what was equivalently the position of a Uniate church for the Church of England. The Archbishop of Canterbury was to receive the pallium from the pope and become a patriarch. Doubtless Cardinal Mercier had good intentions in deciding to read this paper, but he did not realize the trouble it was later to cause. In any case, a deadlock in the Conversations came with Bishop Gore's paper on Fundamentalism ; it showed the absolute cleavage between the views of the two sides on the question of authority. Little more could be done, and even if the death of Mercier and of Portal had not intervened, the fifth Conversation, which was held in October 1926 for the purpose of drawing up a report would have been very little different. Gore and Robinson were also absent and no effort was made to continue the discussions. A Memorandum drawn up by the Catholic side and included in the official report says that in the terminology employed by the Anglicans 'their mind seems throughout all such language to fasten upon a positive conception of a certain power (invested in the pope), rich in its capacity but ill-defined in extent'.([20]) If nothing else had been achieved, this Anglican admission alone would have made the Conversations valuable.

Despite the undoubted good done by the Conversations, there were many unfortunate results, and practically all the personages involved have had to suffer as a consequence. Cardinal Mercier is blamed for not knowing the full facts about the Church of England, or at least of acting as if he did not know them, for he seemed to have the impression that he was dealing with a group of men who were truly representative of the Church of England. 'The largeness of his heart', writes Dr. Frere, 'embraced us all, but his head did not seem to take in our position'.([21]) Cardinal Bourne's biographer is less sympathetic : 'Malines was chosen because Malines was ready to accept the spokesmen from England as typical Anglicans rather than as minority-men whose reading of their Church's character, worship and teaching would have been warmly repudiated by most of their co-religionists at home'.([22]) Mercier's reading of the paper 'L'Église Anglicane unie' was strongly resented by his colleagues of the Catholic delegation, and he had to defend the whole idea of the Conversations in a letter to his clergy. Archbishop Davidson naturally received a good deal of criticism from Protestant quarters, and defended his own attitude to the Conversations in a speech in Canterbury Convocation and in an encyclical letter to the bishops of the Anglican Communion, in which he insisted that the 1920 Appeal to all Christian People was meant also for the Church of Rome.

Despite this, however, we cannot entirely acquit him of the charge of insincerity in relation to the Conversations ; he was afraid of the possible reactions they might have on the Prayer Book Measure which was soon to come before Parliament, and we can sympathize with Lord Halifax in his complaint that 'it is a most painful reflection that Cardinal Mercier should seem more anxious for that reunion, and more ready to consider methods by which it may be brought about, than Your Grace'.([23])

Other unfortunate results followed from the Malines Conversations. From the very beginning, Cardinal Bourne and the English Catholics objected to the holding of such meetings outside of England. It amounted, they claimed, to an admission by the Belgian ecclesiastical authorities that Catholics in England held a different faith from those on the continent. Cardinal Bourne wrote angrily to Cardinal Mercier : 'I have been treated as if I did not exist'.([24]) However justified this attitude may have been, Halifax considered Cardinal Bourne to be the 'villain of the piece', and a further estrangement between English Catholics and the Church of England ensued. Halifax himself caused further unpleasantness in 1930 by publishing the documents of the Conversations despite a previous agreement among all parties that they should not be published. Both Catholics and Anglicans protested against the publication, which was neither correct nor complete. Halifax died before compiling an account of the Conversations parallel to his work on the Anglican Orders controversy thirty years earlier. The Lambeth Conference of 1930 shows no great interest in the Conversations and merely records a faint feeling of regret that they should have been terminated.

Most of the controversy, however, arose from the paper which had been read by Cardinal Mercier at the beginning of the fourth meeting. Its title shows fairly well the thesis put forward in its text : 'L'Église Anglicane unie non absorbée'. It was written by the canonist Dom Lambert Beauduin, and it outlined a scheme for the corporate reunion of the Church of England, under its patriarch the Archbishop of Canterbury, with the Catholic Church. Claiming that 'an Anglican Church absorbed by Rome and an Anglican Church separated from Rome are two conceptions that are equally inadmissible',([25]) it tried to show that historically the position of the English church was that of a national patriarchate united to Rome. It went into great detail about the effect this state of affairs would have on the Catholic Church of the future, dealing at length even with the question of precedence which would arise from the creation of a new patriarch. It insisted that the Code of Canon Law could not be imposed on the English Church, and that the sees founded in 1850 would have to be suppressed eventually. Coming from Cardinal Mercier, the paper naturally appeared to the Anglicans almost too good to be true. 'All this took our breath away', Dr. Frere recalls, ([26]) and it looked as if Roman intransigence were at last breaking down and giving to Anglicans what they always claimed to possess — a place in the Catholic Church.

We must admit that the reading of this paper was a grave error in judgment on the part of Cardinal Mercier. It was read in open violation of an agreement among the Catholic delegation, and both Batiffol and Hemmer insisted that it must not be included in the list of documents of the Conversations. Here again Lord Halifax broke faith and published the paper as part of the proceedings. It cannot be said that it did not contain Mercier's own opinions, for he afterwards wrote to Dom Beauduin who had composed it : 'So, dear friend, thanks to you, we emerge from dreams, we enter at last the domain of realities'. The mere mention of the word 'pallium' was enough to condemn the paper in the eyes of English Protestants, and its ignoring of the doctrinal differences makes it entirely unrealistic.

Corporate reunion as outlined in Dom Beauduin's pamphlet is not entirely opposed to Catholic principles of reunion, for several cases of this type of reunion have occurred even in modern times. What is objected to is the supposition underlying the paper, namely, that at the present time the Church of England is a fit subject for participation in such a reunion project. It is pointed out that Lord Halifax habitually presented his own High Church views as the official teaching of the Church of England. Corporate reunion can take place only where the whole body concerned is a well-defined group ready to accept the whole of Catholic faith and morals. Even the briefest examination will show that the Church of England is in no sense such a unit. The inroads of modernism, the acceptance of semi-pelagianism in theology, the attitude to Christ-

ian morals, as well as many other fundamental differences make
corporate reunion absolutely impossible.

The real emptiness of such a suggestion as that contained in
the paper read by Cardinal Mercier could not have been shown up
better than by the pamphlet read by Bishop Gore during the same
(fourth) Conversation.   He took as his title a phrase from a
work of St. Augustine : 'Concedit (Cyprianus) salvo jure communionis . . . diversum sentire'.   Halifax had denounced Bishop
Gore's appointment to the Anglican delegation as 'a grave blunder',
and at least from Halifax's own point of view the judgment was
correct.   The addition of Gore sharpened the issues and brought
the real points of difference to a head.   The thesis of his paper
was that, just as Cyprian and Pope Stephen had agreed to differ
(diversum sentire) without breaking off communion with one
another (salvo jure communionis) so at the present time the
Church of Rome and the Church of England should agree to
differ on questions of dogma while maintaining full communion
with one another.   Here the distinction of fundamental and non-
fundamental doctrines was brought into play.   'The basis suggested
by the Anglicans', Gore said, 'is the Oecumenical Faith of the
Councils, with a tolerance of diversities determined by the distinction between fundamental and non-fundamental.   This must
be considered a permanent element in the position of Anglicans :
the demand for the distinction will go on'.([27])   The discussion
which followed on the meaning of the terms fundamental and
non-fundamental proved fruitless, for the real point of divergence in the two systems had been reached — the nature of the
act of faith.   Dr. Frere tells us that after Gore's paper the friendly
atmosphere seemed to disappear ; Gore and others as well felt that
'he had said at last, with an explicitness which would have been
previously impossible, what he felt bound to say'.([28])   Gore himself
returned from Malines in a very discouraged frame of mind.

There was a curious consequence to the unauthorized publication of the Malines documents by Lord Halifax in 1930.   He
included the paper 'L'Église Anglicane unie non absorbée', which
was not a part of the Conversations, while he omitted Bishop
Gore's which was.   This seemed all the more strange as Batiffol's
'Réponse au Mémorandum du Dr. Gore' was thus left almost
meaningless.   The whole of the evidence pointed to a deliberate

suppression of Gore's paper by Halifax. He had strongly resented the appointment of Gore to the delegation ; he realized that Gore's paper had terminated the Conversations, and he printed the paper which formed the reply to Gore. Only with the publication of Halifax's biography in 1935-6 did the truth become known. Halifax had either mislaid his copy of Gore's paper or failed to get one at all, and when, in defiance of the agreement that the papers should not be published, he made up his mind to publish them and asked Gore for a copy of his paper, Gore 'indignantly' refused it.([29]) Halifax sent his chaplain to Paris to look for a copy among the papers of the Abbé Portal, but it could not be found and Halifax published the work without it. Thus the estrangement of Gore and Halifax was another result of the Conversations.

The attitude of the Holy See throughout the Conversations was one of bare toleration. It cannot be denied that Cardinal Mercier secured from Rome some form of authorization before the second series of meetings, but the authorization was of the slightest kind. Fr. Congar suggests that it was the paper read by Cardinal Mercier which caused displeasure in Rome ; at any rate, the encyclical *Mortalium Animos,* published in 1928, forbade future meetings with non-Catholics for the discussion of dogma. Once again it explained Catholic doctrine on the nature of the church, and insisted that true reunion consists in the return of all to the one fold. Lord Halifax believed that the encyclical was directed not against the Conversations but against the 1927 World Conference on Faith and Order at Lausanne, but no distinction is made in the Encyclical between Lausanne and Malines — actually many passages have meaning only if taken as referring to the teaching put forward by the Anglican delegation at Malines. For instance, on the subject of the papacy, the encyclical says : 'There are some, though few, who grant to the Roman Pontiff a primacy of honour and even a certain power of jurisdiction ; this, however, they consider to arise not from the divine law but merely from the consent of the faithful'.([30]) The clear rejection of fundamentalism recalls Gore's paper at the Conversations, and many other details leave no doubt that Malines was included in the condemnation. Probably it would have come sooner but for the fact that Cardinal Mercier was alive and was, with Lord Halifax, the prime mover in the holding of the Conversations. The Holy See, however, wished to make sure that there would be no repetition of such meetings between Anglicans and Continental Catholics.

Our fundamental criticism of the Malines Conversations is that, despite the authorisation received from the Archbishop of Canterbury, the Anglican delegation had no right whatever to represent the Church of England as a whole. Representatives of the High Church they may have been, though even that can be disputed ; representatives of the whole Church of England they certainly were not, as is obvious from the actions of other groups in the Church of England about the same time. To take only one example: in 1918 a conference was held between Church of England clergy of the Evangelical Union and leading ministers of the Free Churches. Meetings were again held in the following years, and the two sides agreed to intercommunion and interchange of pulpits, despite the strong protests of the High Church party. This Low Church group had as much — or as little — right to negotiate in the name of the Church of England as had Lord Halifax's High Church group. Further, supposing that instead of Bishop Gore being nominated as an extra member of the Anglican delegation, Dr. Barnes (later Bishop of Birmingham) had been chosen, is it likely that the two sides would have reached fairly close agreement on the subject of the Eucharist ? Bishop Barnes in 1927 issued a challenge to all believers in the Real Presence to accept any form of chemical analysis as a test of their belief. Events showed that Dr. Barnes was quite as representative of the Church of England as the High Church party, for the Archbishop of Canterbury, instead of pronouncing such teaching heretical, contented himself with saying that the Bishop of Birmingham's way of speaking 'gives real offence to the great body of devout Churchmen and Churchwomen'.([31]) The modernist party which Bishop Barnes represented is a part of the Church of England just as much as the High Church and the Low Church, and any schemes for corporate reunion with the Church of England must take all three parties into consideration. At Malines the High Church party put itself forward as fully representative of Anglicanism, and the Catholic delegation accepted it as such. The reports of the Conversations would need to be entirely rewritten if they were to portray faithfully the relations between the Catholic Church and the Church of England. Rather it is far more likely that the Conversations would never have been held if the Low Church and the modernist party had been consulted.

If corporate reunion be impossible for the whole Church of England, we may yet ask : what is the possibility of reunion with the Anglo-Catholic group ? The Anglo-Catholic party is an integral part of the High Church, and the possibility of the High Church abandoning the Church of England in favour of Rome is unthinkable. Besides the strong modernist influence in some sections of the High Church, there is the important factor of the Establishment which binds all the parties together in the one national church. There is the further grave difficulty which we have already discussed namely, the belief that the Church of England is destined to be the 'Bridge' in the reunion of the churches. This idea is as strong in High Church theology as elsewhere, and keeps that party from advancing too far on the road to reunion with Rome lest it prevent a future union with the Eastern Orthodox and with the Free Churches. The number of individual converts from the High Church and particularly from Anglo-Catholicism is certainly very great, but it is not at all likely that the future will see large group conversions to the Catholic Church. The thirty-five years since the Malines Conversations have shown that the existing obstacles are insuperable, and they have actually grown instead of being diminished in that time. The declaration that contraception was lawful, the likelihood that in some parts of the Anglican Communion women will eventually be ordained to the priesthood, the full acceptance of modernism as outlined in the 1938 report on doctrine — all these have added greatly to the difficulties confronting the reunion of the Church of England with the Catholic Church.

It is a rather common Anglican belief that since reunion is out of the question at present because of the dogmatic position, at least co-operation between Anglicans and Catholics should be possible in the social field and especially in the fight against communism. The 1948 Lambeth Conference made an important statement on this subject :

We are conscious of the urgent need of co-operation between Roman Catholics and other Christians on a common ground where ultimate questions of Church order and doctrine which divide us are not raised. We believe that the area, outside the field of faith and order, is very large.

The Committee further pointed to two papal pronouncements on the advisability of such co-operation, and recalled the Joint Letter of Cardinal Hinsley, the Anglican Archbishops, and the Free Church Federal Council in December 1941. This letter contained ten points agreed on by all the parties in relation to the war, five of them being the Five Peace Points outlined by Pius XII at Christmas, 1939. Further co-operation occurred after the war, when a 'Joint Delegation of British Churchmen', including both Anglican and Catholic bishops, visited Germany and issued a report on the state of religion in that country. The Lambeth suggestion that there was a large field where co-operation was possible appeared again in an article entitled 'Catholicism To-day' in *The Times,* suggesting that the relations between the Catholic Church and the non-Catholic bodies could now be re-examined with some advantage to both sides.([32]) The ensuing controversy, while it brought a fair average of 'No Popery' letters, showed a very friendly attitude on the part of some Anglican writers, and a strong plea for co-operation was made by them. In one of the most striking letters contributed during the following month, Bishop Beck, possibly acting as the spokesman of the Catholic bishops of England, pointed out that experience has shown the hope of co-operation along with dogmatic disagreement to be vain. He related how in a whole series of subjects, not directly connected with doctrine, agreement had been sought and could not be reached on even one of them.

With the editorial summing-up of the controversy most people considered that the question had been closed. Hence no little surprise was caused when it was announced in the newspapers a few weeks afterwards that Dr. Prestige, secretary of the Archbishop of Canterbury's Committee for Foreign Relations, was in Rome with a view to implementing the proposals which resulted from the *Times* controversy. The three preliminary points put forward by him are striking, especially the first one, which suggested that the Catholic Church should assume leadership of the reunion movement. In view of the church's attitude to the Ecumenical

Movement, as we shall see, it was quite impossible that this proposal should be even seriously considered. The second suggestion was that an office should be set up in Rome for dealing with reunion problems and for supplying information on the subject. As this proposal would seem to depend on acceptance of the first, it is not of very great importance. Dr. Prestige suggested thirdly that Catholic seminaries should include in their courses some teaching on the position of the non-Catholic denominations and on the reunion movement.

Dr. Prestige later indicated that his visit to Rome was meant to be a continuation of the Malines Conversations. He also stated that the Anglican authorities desired that all questions of dogma should be left until the last and an effort made to concentrate on co-operation in the social field. In view of what we have said about the paper read by Cardinal Mercier at Malines, the decision to let dogmatic differences remain unsettled is unsatisfactory, and Bishop Beck has already shown in the *Times* controversy that agreement upon even one serious matter in the social field is impossible. There did not, then, seem to be much to be gained by Dr. Prestige's visit to Rome.

On December 20th, 1949, the Holy Office issued an Instruction entitled 'De Motione Oecumenica', dealing with the relations between Catholics and non-Catholics, which may perhaps be taken as a reply to Dr. Prestige's proposals. We have, however, no direct evidence of any immediate connection between this document and the Anglican proposals, and as the Instruction deals with the Ecumenical Movement as a whole rather than with relations with the Church of England, we shall postpone our examination of it until we are dealing with that movement.

In view of the continued rejection of the papal claims by the Church of England, a few words on the See of Canterbury may not be out of place here. 'That a Church of nations', wrote Dollinger, 'is not able to maintain itself without a primate, without one supreme head, must be evident to every one ; and history has demonstrated it'.([33]) The extension of the Anglican Communion and the foundation of new national churches in union with the Church of England has tended to make Canterbury the centre of the Anglican world. Another centralising factor has been the holding of the Lambeth Conferences, of which the Arch-

bishop of Canterbury is president, and the result is that Canterbury is gradually assuming the character of a papacy. The change
has not passed unnoticed by Anglicans, and as early as 1908 the
Lambeth Conference recorded the conviction that 'no supremacy
of the See of Canterbury over Primatial or Metropolitan Sees
outside England is either practicable or desirable'. A brief examination of Dr. Bell's fine biography of Davidson will show, however,
that even during Davidson's period of office the process of
centralization was going on very rapidly, and that Davidson was
trying as a matter of principle to carry on almost alone with work
which demanded the assistance of a whole curia. An attempt to
provide the see of Canterbury with such a curia was made at the
1958 Lambeth Conference by extending the duties of the Consultative Body of the Conference so as to give it permanent status.

It is suggested that if ever a complete reunion of non-Catholic
Christians should occur, Canterbury would be the natural centre
for the resulting church or federation of churches. Everywhere,
however, we find such a suggestion deprecated by Anglican
writers ; Swete foresees the creation of new patriarchates, but
he believes that 'a Headship of universal Christendom would be
equally subversive of peace and liberty whether it had its seat
at Constantinople or at Canterbury, at Moscow or at Rome'.([34])
As if to remove all doubts on the matter, the 1948 Lambeth
Conference declared that the churches of the Anglican Communion
do not recognize any peculiar authority as being vested in the
Archbishop of Canterbury but give him merely a 'position of
leadership'. As the Anglican Communion grows, however, the
authority of the Archbishop of Canterbury will grow with it, and
unless some positive steps towards decentralization are taken, Canterbury might well become a papacy in everything but in name.

It is sad to read the many expressions of desire for reunion
with Rome found in Anglican writings and to realize at the same
time the insuperable obstacles which hinder the return of the
Church of England to Catholic unity. Everywhere we find the
feeling of home-sickness and the desire to return. But perhaps
nowhere in Anglican theology do we find that longing for Rome
expressed more beautifully than in one of Bishop Gore's later
works, when the insufficiency of the Church of England was
being more and more borne in upon him, and the glory of the

Catholic Church was attracting him more strongly every day. He wrote :

> As we look towards the great Church of Rome, we know that in the main we Englishmen owe to her our Christianity, and we should delight to acknowledge the primacy of the Bishop of Rome among the churches of Christendom. As we read the record of the separation of the sixteenth century we wonder wistfully whether, if religion had not been so mixed up with politics, and with the passions of imperious monarchs, the separation need have occurred or need have become inveterate. But these are idle dreams ; and as things stand at present no way towards reunion seems to be open . . . We can but wait and pray, in faithfulness to the truth as we see it.([35])

NOTES TO CHAPTER VII

(1) E. C. Messenger, *The Lutheran Origin of the Anglican Ordinal.* See especially pp. 15-27. On the whole question of Anglican Orders, see Francis Clark, *Anglican Orders and Defect of Intention,* which is outstanding for its clarity of presentation.

(2) Mackenzie, *The Confusion of the Churches,* p. 226.

(3) *Lambeth Occasional Reports,* (Latvia and Estonia), p. 247.

(4) J. W. C. Wand, in Mackenzie, *Union of Christendom,* ii. 423.

(5) G. Gillett and W. S. Palmer, *The Claims and Promise of the Church,* p. 38.

(6) H. B. Swete, *The Holy Catholic Church,* p. 20.

(7) In *The Times,* November 10, 1949.

(8) *Doctrine in the Church of England,* pp. 126-7.

(9) G. Johnston, *The Doctrine of the Church in the New Testament,* p. 49.

(10) Gore, *The Holy Spirit and the Church,* pp. 41 ff., 65. On Gore's attitude to St. Peter in the New Testament, see P. Batiffol, *Catholicism and Papacy,* p. 31, and Dom J. Chapman, *Bishop Gore and the Catholic Claims,* p. 50 ff.

(11) F. J. A. Hort, *The Christian Ecclesia*, p. 16.

(12) In Messenger, *Rome and Reunion,* p. 65.

(13) Farrer, in Kirk, *The Apostolic Ministry*, pp. 181-2. It is a grave lack of balance in this work that out of 550 pages it can find only one full page in which to discuss the position of St. Peter, a subject of such immense importance to the thesis of the book.

(14) M. J. Congar, O.P., *Divided Christendom*, p. 33.

(15) M. J. Scheeben, *The Mysteries of Christianity*, p. 553.

(16) A. E. M. Foster, *Anglo-Catholicism,* p. 11

(17) G. L. Prestige, *Charles Gore,* p. 481.

(18) A. R. Vidler, *The Modernist Movement in the Roman Church*, p. 248.

(19) Confusion has been caused by the publication of two distinct sets of documents connected with Malines under the same title. In 1927 there appeared *The Conversations at Malines 1921-1925,* (hereafter called *Malines Report*), which gives the Report signed by the two sides. In 1930 Lord Halifax published *The Conversations at Malines 1921-25,* (hereafter called Halifax, *Malines*) which gives the papers read during the discussions as well as some other documents. Other accounts of the Malines Conversations used here are : Bell, *Randall Davidson*, p. 1254 ff ; J. G. Lockhart, *Charles Lindley, Viscount Halifax*, ii. 265 ff.; E. Oldmeadow, *Francis Cardinal Bourne*, ii. 353 ff ; W. Frere, *Recollections of Malines.* The *opus magnum* on the subject is Jacques de Bivort de la Saudée : *Anglicans et Catholiques,* I : Le Problème de l'Union Anglo-Romaine, 1833-1933. II : Documents sur le Problème de l'Union Anglo-Romaine, 1921-27. (Paris, 1949). Despite the title of the first volume, the writer has very little to say about reunion efforts previous to 1921, and he begins a detailed examination of the Malines Conversations in chapter III. Some hitherto unpublished material is used. The second volume contains practically all the Malines documents in French. The work on the whole is seriously marred by the mis-spellings of English words, as numerous as they are unforgivable.

(20) *Malines Report,* p. 91.

(21) Frere, op. cit., p. 50.

(22) Oldmeadow, op. cit., ii. 362.

(23) Bell, *Randall Davidson,* p. 1277.

(24) Oldmeadow, op. cit., p. 384. The tone of the whole letter is one of unfeigned hostility. Oldmeadow's defence of the attitude of the English Catholics is a very able one, and brings to light much material not available in the other sources. The author had the advantage of writing after the other biographers and freely criticizes them all.

(25) Bell, *Documents,* iii. 27.

(26) Frere, op. cit., p. 56.

(27) *Malines Report,* p. 40.

(28) Frere, op. cit., p. 57.

(29) J. G. Lockhart, *Charles Lindley, Viscount Halifax,* ii. 340.

(30) Text in Messenger, *Rome and Reunion,* p. 75 ff.

(31) Bell, *Randall Davidson,* p. 1323.

(32) *The Times,* October 31, 1949.

(33) J. I. Dollinger, *The Church and the Churches,* p. 37.

(34) H. B. Swete, op. cit., p. 83.

(35) C. Gore, *The Holy Spirit and the Church,* pp. 351-2.

CHAPTER VIII

SCHEMES OF REUNION

In the present chapter we do not intend to examine minutely all the schemes of reunion in which the Church of England has been involved since the beginning of the present century, but we wish to illustrate from some of them the principles of Anglican ecclesiology which we have been discussing. Some of these schemes consisted of conferences between Anglican delegations and representatives of other churches, somewhat like the Malines Conversations ; others, however, were more ambitious and aimed at the immediate corporate reunion of different churches in one area, the result being a single national church in that territory. The first type of reunion scheme has generally not caused much trouble, as usually nothing more is aimed at than mutual recognition and intercommunion, such as was attained at the meeting of the Church of England and the Old Catholic Churches in 1931. The other form, which involves the inclusion of Anglicans in a new national, and therefore non-Anglican, church, has caused several crises each of which has threatened to split the Church of England into opposing camps. We are not concerned here with schemes of reunion in which Anglicans were not involved, for instance the negotiations which led to the formation of the 'United Church of Canada' or the various efforts at reunion among presbyterians.

One of the first and one of the most striking reunion schemes was that which began as a conference on mission 'comity' in British East Africa in 1908. In the following year two further meetings were held, and in June 1913 the conference which was to start the controversy was held at Kikuyu. Four groups were represented — Anglican, Methodist, Presbyterian and an Interdenominational mission. A 'comity' of missions was first agreed upon, and this in itself would not have given rise to any difficulty, but the conference went on to arrange for mutual administration

126

of the sacraments, interchange of pulpits, and a federation on the basis of the 1888 Lambeth Quadrilateral. The proceedings might perhaps have passed unnoticed by the outside world but for the fact that at the end of the conference a united Communion service was held by the Anglican Bishop of Mombasa and all the delegates were invited to take part. Bishop Frank Weston, Anglican bishop of the nearby diocese of Zanzibar, immediately sent a formal protest to the Archbishop of Canterbury, together with an indictment of the bishops of Mombasa and Uganda who had taken part in the united service.([1]) He demanded a trial of the two bishops on a charge of heresy, or at least a public recantation of the doctrinal errors which their action had involved.

The controversy that followed was probably one of the fiercest ever waged in England over a religious question. Pamphlets on both sides were numerous. Bishop Weston himself contributed two important booklets entitled *The Case against Kikuyu*, and *Ecclesia Anglicana : For what does she stand ?* Archbishop Davidson called the three bishops home, and after a number of meetings refused to accept Weston's charge of heresy, referring the dispute to the Central Consultative Body of the Lambeth Conference. This body generally endorsed the ideals and proceedings of the Kikuyu Conference, but insisted that the principles of the Church of England demand that an Anglican should receive Communion from an episcopally ordained minister. The Consultative Body refused to pass judgment on the combined service held at the close of the Kikuyu Conference. Meantime the war had broken out, and when at Easter 1915 Archbishop Davidson in a booklet entitled *Kikuyu* announced his decision, public interest had waned and the crisis was forgotten. He followed closely the opinions of the Consultative Body, refusing to condemn outright anything that had taken place. Another reason why the affair passed off so quietly was the complete change in Bishop Weston's attitude to reunion ; at a further conference held at Kikuyu he addressed the delegates and pressed strongly for the reunion of the different denominations in East Africa. He adopted the same attitude at Lambeth in 1920, much to the surprise of Archbishop Davidson who expected the Kikuyu controversy to flare up again. Weston was strongly in favour of the Appeal to all Christian People, and spent most of his time with the modernist Bishop Henson and with his former opponents, the bishops of Mombasa and Uganda. If he had raised the matter at the Conference, there would almost certainly have been a crisis in the Anglican Communion. He chose, however, to let it drop, though his telegram to the pope from the Anglo-Catholic Congress in 1923 was due to raise a storm of controversy almost as great as that raised by Kikuyu.

After the Lambeth Conference of 1920, further meetings were held in East Africa, but little progress was being made, and by 1920 world interest had moved to the scheme for reunion in South India. In the following years denominational movements among the different churches brought the whole East African attempt at reunion to an end. Kikuyu is, however, no less important because it failed to unite the different churches. It is of supreme importance in the history of the reunion movement because every problem which is appearing to-day in the different schemes appeared many years ago in the Kikuyu controversy. The problem of the ministry was there shown to be the real difficulty in advances to reunion. The position of the episcopate, the status of non-episcopally ordained ministries, the nature of the visible church — these and other fundamental problems all made their appearance in Kikuyu. The attitude first taken up by Bishop Weston of Zanzibar was interesting from the Catholic point of view, for he defended practically the whole of Catholic dogma against what he believed to be the heretical teaching of the other Anglican bishops of East Africa. That he refused to adhere to the doctrine set forth in his indictment and in his two pamphlets undoubtedly averted a crisis, for a continuation of his first stand would have required from the Church of England a definite decision on the position of the episcopate. It is interesting to note that it was the Kikuyu affair that brought the young Ronald Knox into the Catholic Church.

The problem of the ministry is again the main difficulty in the relations of the Church of England with the Church of Sweden. Archbishop Davidson appointed a commission to negotiate with that church in 1909, and two years later its report was published. Nothing further was done until the 1920 Lambeth Conference, when a recommendation was made that the members of the Church of Sweden be admitted to Communion in Anglican Churches, but again a long delay ensued, and we find the 1948 Conference pointing out that the resolution passed twenty-eight years previously had not been formally endorsed by the Convocations and Synods of the churches of the Anglican Communion, and requesting that immediate action be taken in the matter. Part of the delay may be due to the doubt entertained by some Anglicans as to the validity of Swedish orders. When the Archbishop of Canterbury appointed his commission in 1909, the English Church Union held an independent enquiry by means of its own theological committee, and though the investigation resulted in a recognition of the claim to episcopal succession, the theologians taking part were not satisfied as to the intention of the Swedish church in consecrating and ordaining, and the rite employed was also stated to be doubtfully valid. The Swedish church is professedly Lutheran, and its attitude to the episcopal office is well summed up in the oft-quoted phrase of a Swedish bishop that his church possessed episcopacy 'as though we possessed it not'. ([2])

In common with other churches, the Church of Sweden replied to the Lambeth Appeal of 1920, and the paragraphs of this reply dealing with the ministry are illuminating. Despite the fact that the Church of Sweden is an episcopal church claiming apostolic succession, it insisted that for reunion episcopacy was not a necessary prerequisite, and took up a position in regard to the New Testament ministry very much like that put forward by A. C. Headlam in England. It would be interesting to see how an Anglo-Catholic would receive this paragraph of pure Lutheranism :

> No particular organization of the Church and of its ministry is instituted *jure divino,* not even the order and discipline and state of things recorded in the New Testament, because the Holy Scriptures, the *norma normans* of the faith of the Church, are no law, but vindicate for the New Covenant the great principle of Christian freedom. ([3])

Despite the very grave doubts which Anglicans entertain about Swedish sacramental theology — doubts which must have been magnified by this open rejection of New Testament teaching on the ministry — two Anglican bishops took part in Swedish consecrations in Upsala in September 1920, and one Swedish bishop participated in an Anglican consecration in Canterbury in 1927. In 1954 the Convocations of Canterbury and York allowed mem-bers of the Swedish Church to receive Communion at Anglican services, but a very great obstacle to relations between the Church of England and the Church of Sweden has arisen by reason of the recent ordination of three women to the priesthood in the Swedish Church — a step which has renewed the bitter con-troversy which began when the formal decision to ordain women to the priesthood was taken in 1958.

Despite the statement of the 1930 Lambeth Conference that 'it would not, at present, be of any use to approach the Church of Finland', a delegation appointed by the Archbishop of Canterbury and led by Dr. Headlam of Gloucester met representatives of the Church of Finland in Lambeth in 1933 with a view to setting up closer relations between the two churches. Further meetings were held in Finland the following year, and the report which was issued is noteworthy because of the way in which it shows the reactions of Anglicanism on meeting with a Lutheran church. Apparently the Finnish delegation, like many continental Protest-ants, believed that the Church of England was a faithful 'child of the reformation', and asked among other questions : 'What does it involve that many authoritative men in the Church of England have said that the XXXIX Articles are in urgent need of revision ?'(⁴) Dr. Headlam's thinly-veiled Lutheran beliefs assisted the two sides in coming to an agreement, though on the subject of the ministry there were lively exchanges which are worth noting.

The Church of Finland lost whatever claims to apostolic succession it previously possessed in 1884. In that year Professor Granfelt, a priest, 'consecrated' Archbishop Renvall, and from him the whole Finnish hierarchy is descended. No doubts were entertained in Finland at the time about the validity of his action, and the principle has been so admitted into Finnish Canon Law that whenever the bishop of the diocese is not available ordin-ations are carried out by the dean or oldest member of the chapter. The name 'priest' is used, but 'he is not priest in the Roman sense ; no *character indelibilis* is given, and the ordained clergy are in no respect a higher class than the unordained laity'.(⁵) Nor did the Finnish theologians give any guarantee that ordination by a priest would not be carried out in future, and they pointed out that presbyteral ordination was analogous to lay baptism among Anglicans, both being equally valid. On the Anglican side, Dr. C. E. Raven, the noted modernist writer, said that he agreed fully with the conception of orders put forward by the Finnish delegation, and pointed to Article XXXIV of the Thirty-nine Articles in defence of the power of national churches to alter or abolish rites and ceremonies. This conception of the episcopate and priesthood is very different from that put forward as the official Anglican doctrine in the letter to the patriarch of Constantinople in 1922 with a view to the recognition of Anglican orders. Nevertheless the Anglican delegation recommended that mutual episcopal consecrations should take place, that intercommunion should be permitted, and that Finnish bishops should be invited to attend Anglican episcopal conferences. Both Houses of Canterbury Convocation rejected the third recommendation, implying thereby that the members were not satisfied with the orders possessed by the Church of Finland. The Lower House of Canterbury also limited intercommunion to occasions when members of the Finnish church should be cut off from their own ministers. As if to make sure that the Church of England would understand the Lutheran teaching of the Church of Finland, the Archbishop of Turku wrote to the Archbishop of Canterbury in 1936 and said in his letter :

> I must point out that we cannot in principle look upon the historical episcopacy, on which the Anglican Church lays such great stress, as a *conditio sine qua non* for a valid ministry, without abandoning our fundamental doctrinal basis.[6]

So we have here a church which, though it is itself episcopal, is unwilling to agree even to the term 'historic episcopate', let alone any 'theory or interpretation of the fact of episcopacy'. Since 1936, however, Swedish bishops have taken part in Finnish consecrations, and Anglican doubts about the validity of Church of Finland orders will probably disappear, though from the Catholic point of view the ordination and consecration rites of that church, as well as the 'intentio ecclesiae', are obviously invalid.

Conferences held in 1936 and again in 1938 with representatives of the Lutheran churches of Latvia and Estonia followed much the same pattern. The Protestant side of the Church of England was again capably presented by Dr. Headlam, who was able to report to the Archbishop of Canterbury that the delegates were of opinion 'that all three Churches hold the most fundamental doctrines of the Christian Faith'. ([7]) By taking the Thirty-nine Articles as the official Anglican formulary, the two sides were able to reach a fair measure of agreement, though even Low Church theologians would have been alarmed at the positions taken up by the Latvian and Estonian delegations. They insisted on the validity of presbyteral ordinations and of lay celebration of the Eucharist, and pointed out that although the Archbishop of Latvia (himself a member of the conference) had been elected and installed in 1932, he had not taken the trouble to receive episcopal consecration. ([8]) With the other Lutheran churches of Scandinavia we need not deal ; in Denmark, Norway and Iceland the first bishops were consecrated only by priests, and we have already noted the opinion of the 1948 Lambeth Conference that the then recent ordination of women to the priesthood in the Church of Denmark is a serious obstacle to future relations with that church. ([9]) It was decided, nevertheless, to appoint delegations to confer with representatives of these churches.

In complete contrast to these conferences with Lutheran churches is the meeting held between an Anglican delegation and a group of theologians representing the Orthodox Church of Rumania in 1935. Here the 'Catholic' side of the Church of England was presented, and it is noteworthy that the delegation was completely different from the normal group led by Bishop Headlam of Gloucester. From the beginning the Anglicans showed a readiness to concede almost everything to the Rumanian representatives. In reply to a question on the position of the Thirty-nine Articles, it was stated unashamedly that :

> The Doctrine of the Anglican Church is authoritatively expressed in the Book of Common Prayer, and that the meaning of the XXXIX Articles must be interpreted in accordance with the Book of Common Prayer. ([10])

Further, the Anglican delegation unanimously accepted a Rumanian statement on the Eucharist which cannot in any way be reconciled with the official formularies of the Church of England. It strongly asserts the reality of the Real Presence and all but uses the word Transubstantiation. The Anglicans further accepted a Rumanian statement on the nature of tradition which is quite in accord with Catholic teaching, and were not unwilling to give the name Mysteries (musteria) to the five sacraments usually rejected by Protestants. One result of the conference was, as we have seen, that the Orthodox Church of Rumania declared Anglican orders valid in 1936, though the report had already noted that if this course should be decided on, the declaration would be provisional, depending on its being accepted by all the other Orthodox churches.

Such a 'Catholic' presentation of the doctrine of the Church of England was bound to meet with opposition from the Low Church and the modernist sections. When the report was presented to the Upper House of Canterbury Convocation in 1936, Bishop Barnes moved that it be 'received' but not necessarily 'approved', and in the Lower House the opposition was also very strong. Consideration of the document was postponed to the following year, and in the meantime it was denounced by the National Church League, by the Anglican Evangelical Group Movement, and by the 110th Conference of Evangelical theologians. It was again presented to the Convocation of Canterbury in the following year, and was approved 'as being not *the,* but *a* legitimate interpretation of Anglican faith'. The Anglican doctrine of 'facing both ways' was well summed up by Dr. Headlam in a letter to the *Times* during the debates on the Rumanian report. He wrote :

> If there is room for the High Church party in the Church of England there is no doctrinal reason why we should not be in communion with the Orthodox Church, just as if there is room for the Evangelical party there is no doctrinal reason why we should not be in communion with the Episcopal Lutherans. [11]

Since the middle of the last century the Church of England has been trying to set up friendly relations with the sect known as Unitas Fratrum or Moravian Brethren. The Lambeth Conference of 1878 submitted four questions to a group of theologians on the attitude to be adopted with regard to Moravian ministers and ministrations, and a committee appointed in 1906 found the claim of the Unitas to episcopal succession to be 'not proven'. Naturally the Moravians were greatly disappointed that the Church of England should declare their orders invalid, especially in view of the fact that the examination could not have been a thorough one, as it was only after a further report had been presented in 1913 that it was discovered that the Moravians allowed deacons to confirm and to celebrate the Eucharist. The 1920 Lambeth Conference made several sharp demands on the Unitas in matters of doctrine, but little was achieved between that and the next Conference (1930) which pointed out that efforts to unite the two churches went back as far as 1868 and nothing had so far been done to bring them closer together. Further conversations between the two sides could only arrive at 'a mutual agreement to take no further action at present', and the 1948 Lambeth Conference notes that the Archbishop of Canterbury's Committee for relations with the Free Churches has entered into communic- ation with the Moravians and may be able to come to an agreement with them. The 1958 Lambeth Conference adds nothing to previous reports on the situation.

The latest crisis to arise in the Church of England has come as a result of the participation of Anglican bishops and dioceses in the reunion known as the South India Scheme.([12]) In 1908 several small sects had come together to form a united church called the South India United Church (S.I.U.C.), and in 1919 representatives of the S.I.U.C. and the Anglican dioceses in South India met at Tranquebar to discuss the possibility of a national church for South Inlia. An important statement was drawn up at this meeting, insisting that the three elements of church order — Episcopal, Presbyterian and Congregational — must find a place in the new church. The Anglicans asked merely for 'accept- ance of the fact of episcopacy and not any theory as to its character'. The two sides agreed not to call in question the validity of one another's orders, and set up a Joint Committee to promote the cause of reunion. This committee wrote to all the denominations working in South India, but the only group to accept the invitation to reunion were the British Methodists, Despite this initial disappointment the project was not dropped, and the First Preliminary Report was issued in March 1920. In it the purpose of the scheme was clearly outlined as being the formation of a church which would express the Indian religious

spirit, and Bishop Azariah of Dornakal, one of the authors of the
scheme, expressed the same idea in a speech before the Lausanne
Conference in language typically Anglican :

> We want a Church of India, a Church which can be our
> spiritual home, a Church where the Indian religious genius
> can find natural expression, a living branch of the Holy,
> Catholic, and Apostolic Church.[13]

That national feeling was one of the main causes of the movement for reunion in South India is shown by the fact that of
the thirty-three delegates to the original Tranquebar Conference
no less than thirty-one were native Indians.

It would be impossible to give here a detailed account of the
history of the reunion scheme in South India from 1920 onwards,
and we can refer only to the doctrinal issues involved. From the
Anglican point of view the difficulties were immense. The S.I.U.C.,
composed largely of Congregational elements, demanded lay celebration of the Eucharist, and withdrew the demand only under
pressure. Eventually the Anglicans asked for the acceptance of
'Supplemental Ordination' on the ground that at least the authority,
if not the orders, possessed by non-episcopal ministries was incomplete. Years passed and reunion seemed to be as far away as
ever, when suddenly, 'with a rapidity which leaves the student
almost breathless',[14] the union was agreed upon by the negotiating
bodies, and in September 1947 the new 'Church of South India'
came into being.

Since the scheme began in 1919, the reactions in the Church
of England have been very interesting. It was foreseen that one
consequence of the completion of the union would be the loss of
several dioceses of the Anglican Communion, but nevertheless the
Lambeth Conference of 1930 was quite friendly and gave general
approval to the suggestions set forth in the 'Proposed Scheme of
Reunion, 1929'. Nevertheless the Conference pointed out that
the Church of South India would not itself be an Anglican
church, but a distinct province of the church universal. It thereby
refused to accept the suggestion in the Proposed Scheme that
bishops of the new church should be invited to the Lambeth
Conferences, and it offered a number of criticisms of the scheme
with a view to bringing it more into line with Anglican teaching.
The most important position, however, taken up by the confer-

ence was in relation to the non-episcopally ordained ministers of the future church. These, it said, would receive no new standing in the churches of the Anglican Communion, thus implying that they would be accepted in the same way as Free Church ministers. In 1944 the Archbishop of Canterbury (William Temple) wrote to the Metropolitan of the Anglican dioceses in South India and told him that the Church of England would not break off relations with the new church but nevertheless would not be prepared to enter into full communion with it.

By the time the Lambeth Conference met again the Church of South India had become an accomplished fact. A fierce controversy had been fought on the subject in the period after the 1930 Conference and pamphlets appeared in numbers on both sides. Dr. Jalland wrote that the doctrine of the church as set forth in the scheme of reunion was not clear, and stated : 'We seem to be face to face with a deliberate unwillingness to define with any precision a doctrine of the Visible Church'. ([15])   The superiors of a number of Religious Congregations wrote to the Archbishop of Canterbury offering their help in setting up new Anglican dioceses in South India in place of those which had apostatized by joining the new church.   The High Church missionary society (S.P.G.) decided to withdraw entirely from South India, claiming that the scheme had changed substantially since the Lambeth approval of 1930.

The conference of 1948 was far less friendly than its predecessor had been.   It notes that 'grave and deepening anxiety' about the changes in the scheme had caused the Archbishop of Canterbury to appoint in 1946 a committee of theologians to advise him in the matter.   This committee set forth six fundamental criticisms of the proposed Constitution, including charges of ambiguity in the statement of the church's faith and the nature of the sacraments, and it demanded the acceptance of the 'rite' of Confirmation and many other changes.   The Lambeth Conference, having set forth these criticisms and made them its own, refused to enter into full communion with the new church, and said that inter-communion would come only when the Church of South India would possess a ministry unified on an episcopal basis.   Details of partial communion were then set forth, and finally the bishops put forward the two views which were held among them — the first accepting fully the new bishops and priests of the South Indian church, and the second refusing to take any positive action which would imply the validity or invalidity of these orders.

The ministry is again the main difficulty in this scheme of reunion. The Church of South India is pledged to episcopal government and episcopal ordination for the future, but non-episcopally ordained ministers of the uniting bodies were not asked to receive any kind of reordination and they continue to minister to members of the new church, though nominally at least this will be tolerated only for a period of 'growing together' which is to last for thirty years. In order to please Anglicans a guarantee known as 'The Pledge' was given to the effect that a non-episcopal minister would not be forced on an ex-Anglican congregation, but there is no church law safeguarding the pledge and no real guarantee that after the interim period of thirty years non-episcopal ministers will not be permitted to work in the church. The only true bond uniting the parties which formed the union is nationalism, and it was hoped that this would gradually weld into a single unit many elements which teach contradictory doctrines and differ widely in practice. No effort was made to reach dogmatic agreement ; the Scheme of Reunion, as it advanced through the different stages, became more and more vague, so that at present each party is able to interpret it in a sense acceptable to itself. It is a sign, too, of the real character of the new church when we find its official apologia being written by one who holds professedly Lutheran opinions on most of the fundamental Christian doctrines, and who bases his ultimate defence of the South India scheme on the Lutheran doctrine of justification by faith alone, while he propounds a theory of the ministry which is distinctly Lutheran.[16] There seems to be solid ground for the fears of those Anglicans who believe that the new church will be interested only in being a national church without much interest in the faith that it professes.

The position has not changed substantially in the intervening years, and in the meantime attention has turned away from South India to two more ambitious schemes of reunion — the "Scheme" for Church Union in Ceylon (the Church of Lanka) and the "Plan" of Church union in North India and Pakistan. The Lambeth Conference of 1958 recommended these as models for reunion, even though many of the traditional doctrines of Christianity are denied or compromised in both arrangements. It is noted too that the 1958 Lambeth Conference, with the increasing number of such reunions, has become suddenly aware that the creation of a large number of new churches on a purely national basis might result in its own dismemberment (due to the withdrawal of Anglican representatives of these churches from the Conference), and has therefore suggested that bishops of these churches should attend future Lambeth Conferences "as members".

Other schemes of reunion are being prepared in different parts of the world.   Throughout all these schemes there runs the fundamental error of believing that the unity of the church is something human, something which was broken by man's sin and which can be put together again by man's earnestness and zeal.   The principle of nationality, too, is one of the leading ideas in all these schemes.   It is brought forward to justify indifferentism and agnosticism ; and the European missionaries seem so afraid of national feeling that they are prepared to abandon their own faith and join the national church.   The problem of episcopacy has everywhere been by-passed by the distinction between the fact of episcopacy and theories concerning its nature, and there is also the definite refusal to state categorically and unambiguously the relation of the visible to the invisible church. If these be reunions, they are reunions without faith as Catholic theology defines it, and it seems as if we must be prepared to look forward to an age when belief in unequivocal dogmas will be a thing of the past.

NOTES TO CHAPTER VIII

(1) For the text of the protest and indictment, see Bell, *Randall Davidson*, pp. 693-4.

(2) See G. Dix, in Kirk, *The Apostolic Ministry*, p. 301.

(3) Bell, *Documents*, i. 187-8.

(4) *Lambeth Occasional Reports* (Finland) p. 126.

(5) Ibid, pp. 155-6.

(7) *Lambeth Occasional Reports*, (Latvia and Estonia), p. 211.

(8) Ibid., p. 218. This was still true in 1948 ; see *Lambeth Conference 1948*, ii. 76.

(9) See above, Chapter VI.

(10) *Lambeth Occasional Reports* (Rumania), p. 196.

(11) Quoted in Messenger, *The Reformation, the Mass, and the Priesthood*, ii. 655-6. Note that even Dr. Headlam does not suggest that the Church of England should be in communion with the *non-Episcopal* Lutherans.

(12) For the history of the scheme, see *Towards a United Church*, pp. 75-148. For a short account, see Rev. W. J. Hegarty, 'The latest crisis in Anglicanism : the South India Scheme', in I.E.R., 5th. series, vol lxx, no. 1 (January 1948), p. 1 ff. The literature on the subject is now enormous.

(13) E. S. Woods, *Lausanne, 1927*, p. 46.

(14) S. C. Neill, in *Towards a United Church*, p. 138.

(15) T. G. Jalland, *The Bible, the Church and South India*, p. 49.

(16) The apologist is J. E. L. Newbigin, *The Reunion of the Church*. The invisible church is one of the central points of his theology. For his doctrine on justification by faith alone, see p. 84 ff.

CHAPTER IX

THE ECUMENICAL MOVEMENT AND THE FUTURE CHURCH

The foregoing pages have given little or no hint that outside of and independently of the individual efforts at reunion which we have been discussing there is in operation a vast scheme for the ultimate unification of all the churches of the world. Entirely a creation of the present century, the Ecumenical Movement has within the space of about fifty years become the most important element in reunion, and it is safe to say that the rest of this century will see advances in world reunion which will make past reunions seem trivial in comparison. The immediate aim of the Ecumenical Movement is to bring together in conferences all Christian bodies irrespective of their faith and practice, and to get from the assembled delegates an agreed statement on matters of faith, order, and social co-operation. By this method of procedure it is hoped that ultimately differences which separate the various denominations from one another will tend to disappear, and the road will thus be open for the unification of Christ's church into a great church in which all will be brethren and unity will no longer be a vision but an actuality.

Like the Lambeth Quadrilateral, the idea of an ecumenical conference of Christian Churches originated in the Protestant Episcopal Church of America, where a resolution was passed in October 1910 suggesting that the different churches should about making preparations for such a conference. The great World Missionary Conference, held in Edinburgh the same year, gave a definite impetus to the movement, and in reply to the appeal of the American Episcopal Church, practically all denominations set up committees to deal with questions of reunion. It was thus that the first meetings, which we have already noted, came to be held between the Church of England and the Free Churches. In 1919 a deputation was sent to Europe from the

American Church in order to make preparations for a world conference, the general topics of discussion to be 'Faith and Order'. A preliminary meeting was held in Geneva in 1920 and about eighty of the larger denominations sent representatives. The subjects committee met at Oxford in 1923, but it was not until 1927 that the final arrangements were completed, and in that year the first Conference on Faith and Order met in Lausanne with 500 delegates present from churches all over the world.

Meanwhile a parallel and complementary movement to the 'Faith and Order' movement was taking shape, largely under the direction of Nathan Solderblom, Archbishop of Upsala. This movement, later to be known as 'Life and Work', was meant to bring Christians of different denominations together not on questions of dogma but on matters of co-operation in the social and economic field. Thus while Faith and Order took care of dogma and ministry, Life and Work put dogma entirely in the background and endeavoured to bring the churches together for common action. Anglicans, especially the High Church section, seemed to be suspicious of the Life and Work Movement, led as it was by a Lutheran-modernist eclectic, and Dr. Bell gives an amusing account of how Archbishop Davidson discreetly refused to discuss the subject with Soderblom in 1921.[1] A conference eventually met in Stockholm in 1925 under the title 'The Universal Christian Conference on Life and Work'. Very little agreement was reached, the delegates contenting themselves with an official 'Message' of general findings. A second meeting of Life and Work was held in Oxford in 1937 under the title 'World Conference on Church, Community and State', and its report stated that 'a special ground of faith and courage amid the perplexities of our age is that the Christian Church is becoming truly ecumenical',[2] whatever the conference may have meant by the 'church' in this passage. It is interesting to note that when Hitler invaded Russia in 1941 he took with him as proposed patriarch of the Russian church the Orthodox Bishop Serafim who had protested against the holding of this conference on British territory.[3]

The ecumenical movement for reunion took on other forms besides 'Faith and Order' and 'Life and Work'. The 1910 World Meeting of the International Missionary Council at Edinburgh was followed by other similar conferences at Jerusalem (1928), Madras

(1938-9), and at Whitby, Ontario (1947). World Conferences of Christian Youth met at Amsterdam in 1939 and in Oslo in 1946. While all these meetings were concerned at least indirectly with promoting the cause of world reunion, we shall get a clearer view of the whole movement and particularly of the Anglican attitude towards it by an examination of one of them, and for that purpose we shall deal with the one which is generally recognized to have been most influenced by Anglican ideas in its preparation and in the actual meeting — the first Conference on Faith and Order held in Lausanne in 1927.(⁴)

The purpose of the Lausanne Conference was not primarily to set forth the conditions of reunion or to arrange for the unification of the different churches ; its object was 'to register the apparent level of fundamental agreements within the Conference and the grave points of disagreements remaining'. The procedure adopted was that delegates in turn should deliver short speeches which would be made available to all and used as a basis for reports. These reports were then 'received' by the whole conference or 'sent back' for further drafting by the sections. Seven reports in all were drafted, but we are interested mainly in the two which directly concern the church.

The first of the two reports dealing with the church was entitled 'The Nature of the Church,' and the committee set up to report on this heading was composed of 11 Eastern Orthodox, 21 Anglicans, 2 Baptists, 2 Disciples of Christ, 2 Friends (Quakers), 15 Lutherans, 28 Presbyterians and Continental Reformed, and 15 Methodists and Evangelical Church of Germany. From such a heterogenous group, little agreement could be expected. The speeches, too, which were meant to form a basis for the reports, were poles apart on the fundamentals of doctrine. The first speech delivered was by Chrysostom, the Orthodox Archbishop of Athens, and with very little change it could have been from the pen of a Catholic theologian. It laid down clearly and unambiguously the four notes of the visible church, and showed that heretics and schismatics are outside the church and cannot affect its unity. As if to provide a contrast to this 'Catholic' teaching on the church, the next speaker was Dr. S. Parkes Cadman, an American Congregationalist, who was 'elastic, broad, tolerant, inclusive, where the other had been stiff and unyielding. He saw marks of the Church wherever he looked'. A further contrast was afforded by the third speaker, a Lutheran, who emphasized as the fundamental belief of Christianity that 'the church is essentially spiritual' or invisible, and that dogmas are to the church as clothes are to a man — ever-changing. Finally, the bishop of Manchester, speaking as a member of the 'Bridge-Church', sought to reconcile the preceding speeches in a truly Anglican effort at compromise.(5)

The report based on such contradictory points of view could not fail to be vague and ambiguous.   It first sets forth six characteristics which, it claims, make the true church known to men, and then acknowledges that these notes are useless by admitting that the writers differ on the subject of 'the nature of the Church visible and the Church invisible, their relation to each other, and the number of those who are included in each'. Quite obviously, then, these six characteristics do not mark off the true church, as the delegates admit that they themselves do not know what the church is. They proceed next to give details of their differences on the subject of the visible and the invisible church. The section is worth quoting :

1.   Some hold the invisible Church is wholly in Heaven; others include in it all true believers on earth, whether contained in any organization or not.

2.   Some hold that the visible expression of the Church was determined by Christ Himself, and is therefore unchangeable; others that the one Church under the guidance of the Holy Spirit may express itself in varying forms.

3.   Some hold that one or other of the existing Churches is the only true Church ; others that the Church as we have described it is to be found in some or all of the existing Communions taken together.

4.   Some, while recognizing other Christian bodies as Churches, are persuaded that in the providence of God and by the teaching of history a particular form of ministry has been shown to be necessary to the best welfare of the Church ; others hold that no one form of organization is inherently preferable ; still others, that no organization is necessary.

It was at this early stage of the proceedings that the Orthodox delegation withdrew entirely from the voting on the ground that the report was a compromise between contradictory points of view. To one reading the report now, however, it seems like an effort to give full expression to every possible point of view rather than a compromise intended to cover them all under one vague formula.

One would think that after such complete disagreement the conference would have kept reasonably clear of the subject of the church. The matter was brought up again, however, the title of the report this time being 'The Unity of Christendom in relation to existing churches'. After a heated debate, the report, as put forward by the section responsible for its formulation, was rejected by the conference. It is significant that this report was presented by the Archbishop of Armagh, was seconded by Dr. Headlam of Gloucester, and was rejected mainly through the efforts of Anglo-Catholic representatives, which shows that the real nature of the division in Lausanne was along Catholic-Protestant lines. A revised report was later drawn up and presented to the Continuation Committee, but this document is so vague and indefinite that nobody could find any fault with it on dogmatic grounds.

The attitude of the Catholic Church to the Lausanne Conference was clear from the beginning. Although the pope received the American committee which had come to Europe to prepare for the conference, the Holy See refused to have anything to do with the meeting. Further, a decree of the Holy Office dated July 8, 1927, declared that it was unlawful for Catholics to be present at or to countenance conferences with non-Catholics without permission from the Holy See.([6]) Even bishop Gore was quite unenthusiastic about Lausanne, both in his speech at the conference and in his evaluation of its results.

The Continuation Committee of Lausanne met in Prague in 1928 and in Maloja in 1929, and a second World Conference on Faith and Order was held in Edinburgh in 1937. As if to bring into greater prominence the differences of opinion at Lausanne, the Archbishop of York in his opening address told the delegates that the doctrine of the church had not yet received sufficient examination from the Ecumenical Movement.([7]) The treatment given to the subject at the Edinburgh conference was no more satisfactory than that of its predecessor. The church was first defined as 'the Body of Christ and the blessed company of all faithful people', and the report went on to say that 'the invisible Church and the visible Church are inseparably connected though their limits are not exactly coterminous', without, however, making any effort to say what those limits were.   Some of the delegates insisted on the use of the term 'invisible church', while others regarded it as misleading and unscriptural.   After a fruitless effort to decide what type of future unity the various denomin‑ ations desired, the delegates arrived at a conclusion which should have been obvious from the reports of the Lausanne Conference, namely, that 'behind all particular statements of the problem of corporate union lie deeply divergent conceptions of the church'.

Since 1937 the ecumenical movement has developed rapidly. After the Edinburgh meeting, steps were taken to unify the various movements into one great world‑wide organization, and in 1938 a provisional constitution was drawn up for a proposed World Council of Churches, whose main duty would be to take care of and to co‑ordinate the two movements of 'Faith and Order' and 'Life and Work'.   Archbishop Temple of York wrote to Cardinal Maglione in 1939 on behalf of the World Council and, while noting the unwillingness of the Catholic Church to become a member of the new organization, asked for an exchange of information and for permission for unofficial consultations with Catholic theologians.   The Holy See replied through the Apos‑ tolic Delegate to Great Britain granting the required permission. A conference held in Utrecht in 1939 planned a unified meeting of the various branches of the ecumenical movement for 1941, but the war intervened, and it was not until 1948 that the World Council of Churches held its first meeting at Amsterdam.   The declared purose of the Council was the integration of the 'Faith and Order' and 'Life and Work' movements, along with other ecumenical groups, but it was decided that these bodies were not to be dissolved — they would keep their identity while acting as integral parts of the new organization.   Various subordinate aims of the merger were declared at Amsterdam : the various churches wished to use the Council as a means of getting to know one another better, to co‑operate with one another in the social field and on mission work and to call world conferences on particular Christian problems from time to time.

Amsterdam was a great achievement for the non-Catholic bodies. Its importance lies in this that the delegates were present no longer as individual persons but as representatives of their various churches, and for the future one single world-wide body could speak on behalf of all Christendom — that is, with the single exception of the Catholic Church — among the major Christian bodies. From the beginning, however, the World Council of Churches made it clear that it did not pretend to be the Church of Christ : it emphasised that it was not the Church but a Council of Churches.

Since the first meeting at Amsterdam there has been some event of note each year. In 1949 there was a meeting in Bangkok sponsored by the World Council of Churches and the International Missionary Council. It was a meeting of the Missionary Churches in Asia and the main idea put forward at the meeting was that the divisions in Christendom reflect the old European disagreements which are quite outmoded to-day. There was a clear call at Bangkok for the abandonment of dogmatic differences and a general plea for reunion among the members of the Council.

It had been arranged at Amsterdam that there would be an annual meeting of the committee of the World Council. In 1950 at Toronto a very important statement was issued on the subject of membership of the Council. It stated that for the future any church could continue to be a member of the Council without admitting that the other members belong to the true Church at all. It would appear that this was aimed primarily at keeping the Eastern Orthodox in the Council but there is also the probability that it was intended as an invitation to the Catholic Church to come in.

In 1952, a conference of the 'Faith and Order' movement — now a Commission of the World Council of Churches — met at Lund in Sweden. It was intended to be a continuation of the Lausanne Conference of 1927 but it was now fully sponsored by the World Council of Churches. As at Lausanne, the division of opinion between the members of the movement was clearly on the basis of a Catholic versus a Protestant concept of the Church. At the same time there was a very strongly worded statement issued on the doctrine of the Eucharist as 'the sacrifice we offer'. This sacrificial aspect of the Eucharist appears clearly for the first time and is perhaps indicative of at least one group within the World Council itself moving towards a Catholic view of the Church.

In 1954, at Evanston, a further meeting of the whole World Council of Churches was held with about 600 delegates attending from 163 denominations. Little, however, was done at Evanston as the organisers seemed to fear that the Council might break up if controversial issues were chosen. The primary theme was 'Christ the Hope of the World' and it had been thought that this theme might limit the work of the meeting to the question of social co-operation. The secondary theme (one of six) was reunion, and from a Catholic point of view the discussion here was very disappointing in that the unity of the Church and the Church itself were both defined as invisible and it was declared that it was a matter for the Churches themselves to decide what kind of unity they wanted. This would imply, of course, that Christian unity is something man-made, not something God- given. It was also disappointing to find that claims by delegates from behind the Iron Curtain that there was religious freedom there were allowed to go unchallenged. The next meeting of the World Council of Churches is scheduled for New Delhi in November-December, 1961, the general theme being "Jesus Christ, the Light of the World", with three sections entitled Unity, Witness and Service. The year 1961 may well be a very important one from the point of view of reunion, as it is likely that a Pan-Orthodox meeting will be held towards the end of the year to discuss the theme of Christian unity, and both the World Council of Churches and the Pan-Orthodox Synod will have their eyes on the Second Vatican Council which will follow soon after.

With the theology of the Ecumenical Movement in general we are not concerned here. We are interested only in the fact of Anglican participation in the movement and the theology of the church that this participation involves. So far, at least, we can say that, with the exception of some Anglo-Catholics, Anglicans in general have cause to be satisfied with the course which ecumenism is taking. The 'Bridge-Church' is quite at home in a milieu which is a mixture of Catholic and Protestant principles, and it delights in finding itself to be the *via media* between opposing groups. In virtue of its 'comprehensiveness' the Ecumenical

Movement is simply the Church of England on a large scale, containing in one organisation the deep Protestantism of the Lutheran sects and the Catholicism of Eastern Orthodox and Anglo-Catholics. The same tension exists as in the Church of England, ever threatening to dissolve the union into its component parts, and yet managing somehow to keep them all together within the bounds of one compact organisation. The Ecumenical Movement is certainly the actualisation of Anglican ideals, and will in the future owe practically everything to Anglican interest and enterprise.

The Ecumenical Movement itself scarcely calls for detailed criticism. The published reports of the different conferences — and particularly the Lausanne Conference — are sufficient criticism. Fr Congar in a magnificent chapter[8] examines critically the theories on which the movement is based, and Jenkins sums up his criticism as 'devastating'.[9] The movement is, we concede, in its infancy, and it can hardly be expected to have its theological principles clear-cut and exact, but it is obvious even now that time will not remove the disagreements between the various churches which are taking part in it. The differences are deep and fundamental, and the only agreement that will ever be reached will be agreement to disagree. 'How so great a variety of opinions', wrote Pius XI, 'can clear the way for the unity of the Church, we know not'.[10] Compromise and comprehension may bring an apparent measure of agreement, but no assembly such as the World Council of Churches can ever hope to bring about agreement on church unity when the parties do not know what they mean by the church and what they mean by unity. The request by Dr. Prestige during his recent visit to Rome that the Catholic Church should assume the leadership of the reunion movement showed a deep lack of realization of the teaching of the church.

On December 20, 1949, the Holy Office issued an Instruction 'De Motione Oecumenica'.[11] It opens with the simple statement of fact that the Catholic Church does not take part in conferences of the Ecumenical Movement, but says that nevertheless this world-wide desire for reunion 'is certainly a cause of holy joy in the Lord to the sons of the True Church'. It repeats the Catholic doctrine on church reunion, and declares that the teaching of the three encyclicals on the church (*Satis Cognitum, Mortalium Animos, Mystici Corporis*) is still in force. In relation to the holding of reunion conferences, it allows the bishop for a period of three years to give permission for the holding of diocesan reunion meetings, and permits the common recitation of the Our Father or other authorised prayers at such gatherings. The whole instruction is guarded and conservative, and the Archbishop of York, Dr. Garbett, was not far wrong when he said it was 'restrictive rather than permissive'.([12]) The Holy See is rightly conservative in its dealings with the Ecumenical Movement, though the setting up of a secretariat for Christian Unity under Cardinal Bea in June, 1960, will undoubtedly bring closer contacts.

Is it possible, we may ask, that we shall one day find the world divided into two great churches, the one Roman and the other non-Roman ? The union of non-Roman Christians among themselves, if only the union be sincere, is undoubtedly something over which we must rejoice, as the Holy Office Instruction says, though the results to the Catholic missions, for example, may not be to our advantage. An anonymous writer thinks that this process of unification of all non-Catholic sects will take less time than separates us from the reformation, and considers this to be the preparation for the final reunion of the whole world in the one Catholic Church.([13]) Baron von Hügel also considered that these non-Catholic unions would tend ultimately to the reunion of all Christendom. When we look, however, to the continued multiplication of sects since the reformation, and when we examine the ever-increasing number of religious denominations in the world to-day, we are led to the conclusion that despite the desire for unity shown by those participating in the Ecumenical Movement, the rejection of the authority of the Catholic Church tends to begin a process of 'protesting' which ends in rejection of all external authority in religion and makes every man his own authority, his own church. There is no *via media* between an authoritative infallible church and absolute unrestricted private judgment.

The real test of the Ecumenical Movement lies in its vision of the future church at which it is aiming, and Anglican hopes of unity can be judged by the same standard. In the Lambeth

Appeal of 1920 the bishops of the Anglican Communion put forward as their ideal

> a Church, genuinely Catholic, loyal to all Truth, and gathering into its fellowship all 'who profess and call themselves Christians', within whose visible unity all the treasures of faith and order, bequeathed as a heritage by the past to the present, shall be possessed in common, and made serviceable to the whole Body of Christ.

At Lausanne a serious effort was made to draw a picture of the future ecumenical church, and though the report containing it was not accepted by the conference it can be taken as representative of the Ecumenical Movement, and it will serve as a useful basis for an examination of the Anglican and Ecumenical outlook on the church of the future.

The first note of the great future church is, we are told, 'a common Faith, a common Message to the world'. In itself, the statement can be taken in a perfectly orthodox sense, namely that the church of Christ must have one apostolic faith which it teaches to the whole world without distinction of persons. The Catholic Church has always claimed to preach such a faith and such a message to the world. But what did this phrase mean at Lausanne ? It meant what it has always meant in Anglican theology — the doctrine of fundamentalism combined with the doctrine of the autonomy of national churches. The future church will have a common message certainly, but it will be a common message 'based upon common fundamental beliefs', and it will be sent forth from a church 'assembled on a plan of autonomy and fellowship similar to that which is the basis of our Conference to-day'. We have already shown that the doctrine of fundamentalism while plausible enough in theory, fails when applied in practice, and yet it is the real source of both Anglican and ecumenical theology for the future church. Again, we have no guarantee of the future church's attitude towards Modernism. Anglican theology has already fallen a victim to it. Of its ultimate triumph, Dr. Barnes tells us, there can be no question,([14]) while from the Anglo-Catholic side it is admitted that at the present time it is the most active enemy. The Ecumenical Movement is similarly honeycombed with modernist principles, due

both to English modernism and the personal influence of Soderblom, and it is quite likely that the 'common Faith and common
Message' of the future church will be based on modernism as
well as on fundamentalism.

The second characteristic of the future church is to be the use
of the rite of baptism as incorporating members into the one
church. This condition of membership would certainly be rejected
by the Society of Friends, which is at present accepted as part of
Christ's church both by Anglicans and by the Ecumenical Movement. Nor could any agreement ever be reached as to the age
for baptism, for the Baptists stand for one principle — baptism of
adults only. The meaning of baptism is left entirely vague, and
the uniting churches would be quite free to accept any interpretation of its significance that pleased them, accepting or rejecting
at will the whole doctrine of original sin and redemption. The
third note of the church is equally vague — 'Holy Communion
as expressing the corporate life of the Church and its signal act
of corporate worship'. An effort is obviously being made in this
sentence to express the double nature of the Eucharist as sacrament
and sacrifice, while at the same time avoiding carefully anything
that might offend Protestant ears. In regard to both parts of the
phrase, absolute freedom of interpretation is allowed. As it stands,
it could cover every type of teaching from transubstantiation to
receptionism and virtualism, and the second half could apply
equally well to the Catholic doctrine of the Mass and the Lutheran
repudiation of a Eucharistic sacrifice.

We may take together the fourth and fifth 'characteristics' of
the future church. The fourth claims for the ecumenical church
'a ministry accepted throughout the universal church', while the
fifth insists on 'freedom of interpretation about Sacramental grace
and ministerial order and authority'. The combination of these
two elements is reminiscent of the acceptance of the historic
episcopate with the rejection of any implications about theories
as to its nature. Due to the influence of the Lutherans and the
Free Churches, the 'historic episcopate', for all its vagueness, was
not acceptable at Lausanne, and the resultant compromise, 'a
ministry accepted throughout the universal church', means little.
As if to make sure that there were no 'sacerdotal' theories implied

in the fourth note, the fifth demanded complete freedom of interpretation on the subjects of grace, order and authority.

The last element of the future church is particularly interesting :
it asks for 'due provision for the excercise of the prophetic gift'.
The High Anglican interpretation of 'due provision' in this phrase
would probably amount to a denial of the whole proposal, while
for the Free Churches (who were responsible for its insertion)
it could be extended to cover lay preaching and lay celebration
of the Eucharist. It is an indication of the influence of 'non-
sacerdotal' theology in the Ecumenical Movement and shows that
many of the churches are refusing to abandon a 'prophetic' ministry
in favour of a sacerdotal or episcopal one. This acceptance of
the two types of ministry on an equal basis is, for Newbigin and
others, the real starting-point of Ecumenical theology.[15]

In these suggested characteristics of the future church no
mention is made of unity, and it is left to our imagination to
picture what type of unity the ecumenical church will possess.
It will not be a 'vast Christian super-organisation, rigid and in-
flexible, dominating the whole Christian Church'.[16] In moments
of enthusiasm the Lambeth Conferences have pictured the Anglican
Communion as a temporary, transitional arrangement, longing for
and preparing itself for the day when it can lose itself in the
unity of the Catholic Church of the future, but we cannot imagine
English nationalism bowing down before any international body
without a fundamental change in the Anglican idea of the national
church. Slosser believes that the basis for the future union of
Christendom will have to be very simple, with full provision for
different doctrines and interpretations, the final result being, as he
says, 'a deeply spiritual, Evangelical, constitutional, Congregational,
Presbyterial, cosmopolitan Christian Catholicism'(!) [17] It would
seem to be more reasonable to reject this pitiful wishful thinking and
to conclude that 'there is no sign of any universal and complete
unity in this world'.[18]

Of the nature of the great future church, the Catholic Church
alone can speak with clarity and certainty. Visible in its unity
since the first century, it will continue to be visibly one until the
end of time, while sects and denominations fail to agree whether
the visible church should be one or whether the one church should
be visible. In doctrine there will be a continuation of the same

legitimate development, with perhaps further definitions clarifying the content of the *depositum fidei*. There will be no new doctrines in the strict sense, and no withdrawal of doctrines already defined. There will, perhaps, be a greater variety in liturgy and national customs, and any groups which return to the church will no doubt be granted a wide degree of tolerance in questions not pertaining to the faith. But there can be no compromise on revealed truth, and the dogmatic decrees of Trent and the Vatican Council would have to be accepted in all their fulness.

The loss of the Anglican world to the Catholic Church has been an irreparable one. It occurred at a time when England was about to begin its great era of colonization, and the four hundred dioceses of the Anglican Communion to-day give us some idea of what might have been done for Catholic missions if England had remained faithful. Theologically, too, the loss was immense. If Anglicans object that the development of the notion of authority in the Catholic Church has been one-sided, one must point out to them that their continuance in schism may be the real cause of further differences between the two bodies. Revelation does not guarantee to us that the whole world will one day be in the Catholic Church, whatever interpretation we may give to St. Paul's mysterious phrase about the 'fulness of the gentiles' being converted, and it may perhaps be true that the church is destined, as the Chosen People of old, to be restricted to a 'remnant'. Whatever the future before her, the Catholic Church will ever remain what her Divine Founder made her to be — One, Holy, Catholic, Apostolic, founded upon the Rock that is Peter.

NOTES TO CHAPTER IX

(1) Bell, *Randall Davidson,* p. 1048 ff.

(2) Bell, *Documents,* iii. 244.

(3) E. Rosenstock-Huessy, *The Christian Future,* p. 158 note.

(4) M. J. Congar, O.P., *Divided Christendom,* p. 131 : 'Lausanne was a characteristic product of the Anglican outlook'. For the official reports, see H. N. Bate, (Ed.), *Faith and Order, Lausanne, 1927.* E. S. Woods, *Lausanne 1927,* describes itself as a 'quasi-official and popular' interpretation of the Conference. The reports are also given in G. J. Slosser, *Christian Unity : its History and Challenge,* p. 396 ff., and in Bell, *Documents,* ii. 1. ff.

(5) Text of these speeches is in Bate, op. cit., p. 106 ff.

(6) *A.A.S.,* vol. XIX., p. 278.

(7) T. O. Wedel, *The Coming Great Church,* p. 79.

(8) Congar, op. cit., chapter IV : The Theories underlying the "Ecumenical Movement", p. 115 ff.

(9) Jenkins, *The Nature of Catholicity,* p. 129. It is a striking tribute to Congar's book that he gets the highest praise from High Church writers like Hebert, Bell, Mascall and F. W. Green, as well as from Protestants like Jenkins and Newbigin.

(10) *Mortalium Animos,* in Messenger, *Rome and Reunion,* p. 83.

(11) Text in *A.A.S.,* vol XLII, pp. 142-7.

(12) Diocesan Letter, quoted in *The Times,* March 27, 1950.

(13) *A Spiritual Pilgrimage towards the Threshold of the Catholic Church,* p. 139.

(14) E. S. Barnes, *Should Such A Faith Offend ?,* p. 270.

(15) J. E. L. Newbigin, *The Reunion of the Church,* p. 187.

(16) W. J. Noble, in *Towards a United Church,* p. 9.

(17) Slosser, op. cit., p. 366. This statement is put forward in all seriousness as a picture of the future church.

(18) J. J. Willis, in *Towards a United Church,* p. 203. Thus also Cadoux, *Catholicism and Christianity,* p. 649 : 'Visions, therefore, of a reunited Christendom . . . resemble not so much the distant heights of a slope we have already begun to climb, but rather a far point in space whither neither feet nor wings can carry us.'

EPILOGUE

This book was already in the hands of the printers when Dr. Fisher, Archbishop of Canterbury, visited His Holiness Pope John XXIII in December, 1960. Both sides emphasised that the visit was nothing more than a courtesy call, and that no positive step towards reunion would result from it. Nevertheless it was agreed by all observers that the visit was a most important one.

Like every other event in history, this visit can be rightly understood only in the context in which it took place. It would be foolish to interpret it as an act of submission by the head of a schismatic church, though some would see in it the beginning of a process that might ultimately lead to submission ; and it would be equally incorrect to interpret the visit as a major concession forced from the Holy See through the influence of the Ecumenical Movement.

In our view, the visit has meaning from the Anglican point of view only in terms of the Bridge-Church idea which an earlier chapter has studied. This was not merely a visit to the Pope. It was a visit to the Orthodox world as well — a visit, in the terms of our metaphor, to the 'Catholic' end of the bridge. That it was undertaken at all is clear proof that Dr. Fisher felt reasonably safe in leaving the 'Protestant' end of the bridge even for a time ; it was a daring visit to this extent that no representative of the Church of England had ventured so near the 'Catholic' end of the bridge before. Still thinking in terms of our metaphor, we can safely conclude that this visit to the 'Catholic' side will be followed by an equally important journey to the 'Protestant' end — that is, to further overtures to the Free Churches and other Protestant groups. In Anglican eyes, the visit to the Pope by Dr. Fisher was another great advance in the fulfilment of the role assigned by providence to the Church of England.

From the Catholic point of view, the visit was no more than a practical acknowledgement of the solicitude of the Chief Pastor for the separated brethren, and a sign that Anglican hostility to the Papacy was at last ended after some four hundred years. Dr. Fisher's visit to Cardinal Bea, head of the Commission for the Promotion of Christian Unity (founded as late as June, 1960) was also an indication of future direct contacts between that Commission and the Ecumenical Movement. Many Catholic ecumenists will be pleased, no doubt, that the new code of Rubrics for the Catholic Church which came into force on 1st January, 1961, changed the votive Mass 'ad tollendum schisma' into 'Missa pro unitate Ecclesiae'.

Ut omnes unum sint !

BIBLIOGRAPHY

Only those works are listed which are quoted, or used directly or indirectly, in the text. Abbreviations of certain titles as used in the notes are explained in the Introduction.

a) OFFICIAL OR SEMI-OFFICIAL PUBLICATIONS :

G. K. A. Bell (Ed.)

Documents on Christian Unity, 1920-1924, Oxford, 1924.

Documents on Christian Unity, Second Series, 1924-1930, Oxford, 1930.

Documents on Christian Unity, Third Series 1930-1948, Oxford, 1948.

Lambeth Reports :

The Six Lambeth Conferences, 1867-1920, S.P.C.K., 1929.

The Lambeth Conferences (1867-1930), S.P.C.K., 1948.

Lambeth Conference, 1948, S.P.C.K., 1948.

The Lambeth Conference, 1958, S.P.C.K. and Seabury Press, 1958.

Lambeth Occasional Reports 1931-8, S.P.C.K., 1948.

Lambeth and You, S.P.C.K., 1948.

Doctrine in the Church of England, S.P.C.K., 1938.

The Canon Law of the Church of England, S.P.C.K., 1947.

The Conversations at Malines 1921-1925, Oxford, 1927.

Lord Halifax (Ed.), *The Conversations at Malines 1921-25,* London, 1930.

L. Hodgson, *The Doctrine of the Church as held and taught in the Church of England,* Oxford, 1946.

H. N. Bate (Ed.), *Faith and Order, Lausanne, 1927,* London, 1927.

E. S. Woods, *Lausanne 1927,* London, 1927.

Dunkerley (Ed.), *The Ministry and the Sacraments,* London, 1937.

Evanston Speaks : Reports from the second Assembly of the World Council of Churches, London, 1955.

b) ANGLICAN WORKS :

E. W. Barnes, *Should Such a Faith Offend* ?   London, 1927.

G. K. A. Bell, *Randall Davidson,* Oxford, 1938 (2nd ed.)
  Christian Unity, London, 1948.

E. J. Bicknell, *A Theological Introduction to the Thirty-nine Articles,* London, 1942 (New edition, revised by H. J. Carpenter).

Alfred Blunt, *What the Church Teaches,* Penguin publications 1942.

Z. N. Brooke, *The English Church and the Papacy,* Cambridge, 1931.

C. P. S. Clarke, *The Via Media,* London, 1937.

C. M. S. and Church Union in South India, London, 1947.

T. S. Eliot, *Selected Essays,* London, 1934 (2nd ed.).

A. E. M. Foster, *Anglo-Catholicism,* London, 1914.

W. Frere, *Recollections of Malines,* London, 1935.

G. Gillett and W. S. Palmer, *The Claims and Promise of the Church,* London, 1910.

Charles Gore, *The Incarnation of the Son of God,* London, 1891.
  The Holy Spirit and the Church, London, 1924.
  Christ and Society, London, 1928.
  Dominant Ideas and Corrective Principles, London, 1918.
  (Ed.) *Lux Mundi,* London, 1913 (15th ed.).

H. L. Goudge, *The Church of England and Reunion,* S.P.C.K. 1938.

Lord Halifax, *Leo XIII and Anglican Orders,* London, 1912.

R. S. T. Haslehurst, *Church of England Doctrine,* 2 vols., S.P.C.K., 1938.

A. C. Headlam, *The Doctrine of the Church and Christian Reunion,* London, 1920.

A. G. Hebert, *The Form of the Church,* London, 1944.
  Memorandum on the Report of the Archbishops' Commission, S.P.C.K., 1939.

G. F. Holden, *The Special Bases of the Anglican Claim,* London, 1903.

F. J. A. Hort, *The Christian Ecclesia,* London, 1897.

J. W. Hunkin, *Episcopal Ordination and Confirmation in relation to Intercommunion and reunion.* Cambridge, 1929.

W. R. Inge, *The Church and the Age,* London, 1912.

T. G. Jalland, *The Church and the Papacy,* S.P.C.K., 1944.

The Bible, the Church and South India, London, 1944.

C. Jenkins and K. D. Mackenzie (Eds.), *Episcopacy, Ancient and Modern,* S.P.C.K., 1930.

Sheila Kaye-Smith, *Anglo-Catholicism,* London, 1925.

B. J. Kidd, *Documents illustrative of the Continental Reformation,* Oxford, 1911.

K. E. Kirk (ed.), *The Apostolic Ministry,* London, 1946.

T. A. Lacey, *Unity and Schism,* London, 1917.

The Unity of the Church as treated by English theologians, S.P.C.K., 1898.

J. G. Lockhart, *Charles Lindley, Viscount Halifax,* 2 vols., London, 1935-6.

K. D. Mackenzie, *The Confusion of the Churches,* London, 1925.

(ed.) *Union of Christendom,* 2 vols., London, 1938 (Religious Book Club edition).

E. L. Mascall, *Christ, the Christian, and the Church,* London, 1946.

Lambeth 1958 and Christian Unity, London, 1958.

A. J. Mason, *The Church of England and Episcopacy,* Cambridge, 1914.

D. M. McKinnom, *The Church of God,* Westminster, 1940.

C. S. Milford, *South India's New Church,* London, 1947.

P. E. More and F. L. Cross, *Anglicanism,* S.P.C.K., 1935.

J. H. Newman, *Tracts for the Times*: *Tract 90,* London, 1841.

S. L. Ollard, *Reunion,* London, 1919.

E. J. Palmer, *South India,* London, 1944.

G. L. Prestige, *Charles Gore,* London, 1935.

H. Rashdall, *Christus in Ecclesia,* Edinburgh, 1912.

E. C. Rich, *Spiritual Authority in the Church of England,* London, 1952.

E. G. Selwyn, (ed.) *Essays Catholic and Critical,* S.P.C.K., 1912.

Six Oxford Tutors, *Contentio Veritatis,* London, 1902.

B. H. Streeter (and others), *Foundations,* London, 1912.

H. B. Swete, *The Holy Catholic Church,* London, 1919.

N. Sykes, *The Church of England and Non-Episcopal Churches in the sixteenth and seventeenth centuries,* S.P.C.K., 1948.

H. E. Symonds, *The Council of Trent and Anglican Formularies,*
    Oxford, 1933.

(Various Writers) *Towards a United Church,* London, 1947.

A. R. Vidler, *Witness to the Light (The Theology of F. D. Maurice),*
    New York, 1948.
        The Modernist Movement in the Roman Church,
        Cambridge, 1934.

N. P. Williams and C. Harris, *Northern Catholicism, S.P.C.K.,*
    1933.

c)   CATHOLIC WORKS :

Karl Adam, *The Spirit of Catholicism,* London, 1938 (Unicorn
    edition).

Anonymous, *A Spiritual Pilgrimage Towards the Threshold of
    The Catholic Church,* London, 1931.

J. B. Bagshawe, *The Church, or, What do Anglicans mean by
    'the Church'?* London, 1890.

A. S. Barnes, *The Popes and the Ordinal,* London, 1896.

P. Batiffol, *Catholicism and Papacy,* London, 1925.

R. H. Benson, *Non-Catholic Denominations,* London, 1910.

A. Bolton, *A Catholic Memorial of Lord Halifax and Cardinal
    Mercier,* London, 1935.

L. Cerfaux, *La Théologie de l'Église suivant S. Paul,* Paris, 1948
    (2nd ed.)
        L'Église des Corinthiens, Paris, 1946.

Dom. J. Chapman, *Bishop Gore and the Catholic Claims,* London,
    1905.

Francis Clark, *Anglican Orders and Defect of Intention,* London,
    1956.

M. J. Congar, O.P. *Divided Christendom,* London, 1939.

G. Constant, *The Reformation in England,* London, 1942 (Vol. III)

C. Dawson, *The Spirit of the Oxford Movement,* London, 1933.

J. I. Dollinger, *The Church and the Churches, London,* 1862.

C. J. Dumont, O.P., *Approaches to Christian Unity* (trans. H. St.
    John, O.P.), London, 1959.

F. Dvornik, *National Churches and the Church Universal,*
    London, 1944.

D. Fahey, *The Mystical Body of Christ in the Modern World,* Dublin, 1935.

W. J. Fitzpatrick, *Life, Times and Correspondence of the Right Rev. Dr. Doyle,* 2 vols. Dublin, 1861.

J. B. Franzelin, *De Divina Traditione et Scriptura,* Rome, 1896 (4th ed.).

R. Garrigou-Lagrange, *La Synthèse Thomiste,* Paris, 1946.

E. Hanahoe, S.A., *Catholic Ecumenism,* Washington, 1955.

'Father Jerome' (Rev. A. Gille), *A Catholic Plea for Reunion,* London, 1934.

A. Janssens, *Anglicanism,* C.T.S.E., 1945 (revised by E. C. Messenger).

H. J. T. Johnson, *Anglicanism in Transition,* London, 1938.

R. A. Knox, *The Belief of Catholics,* London, 1939 (Unicorn Edition).

C. Lattey, (ed.), *The Church,* Cambridge, 1928.
The Pre-Nicene Church, Cambridge, 1935.

Bernard Leeming, S. J., *The Churches and the Church,* London, 1960.

E. Maguire, *Is Schism Lawful ?* Dublin, 1915.

D. Mathew, *Catholicism in England, 1535-1935,* London, 1936.

Vincent McNabb, O.P., *The Church and Reunion,* London, 1937.

E. Mersch, *The Whole Christ,* Milwaukee, 1938.

E. C. Messenger, *The Reformation, the Mass and the Priesthood,* 2 vols., London, 1936-7.
The Lutheran Origin of the Anglican Ordinal, London, 1934.
(ed.), *Rome and Reunion,* London, 1934.

Rev. W. Moran, *The Government of the Church in the First Century,* Dublin, 1913.

L. O'Donovan (ed.), *Assertio Septem Sacramentorum,* New York, 1908.

E. Oldmeadow, *Francis Cardinal Bourne,* London, 1944. (Vol. II).

F. Prat, *The Theology of St. Paul,* 2 vols., London, 1945.

Arthur H. Ryan, *The Church of Christ,* Dublin, 1949.

M. J. Scheeben, *The Mysteries of Christianity,* St. Louis, 1947.

J. de B. de la Saudée, *Anglicans et Catholiques,* 2 vols. Paris, 1949.

Henry St. John, O.P., *Essays in Christian Unity,* Blackfriars, 1955.

J. L. Stoddard, *Rebuilding a Lost Faith,* London, 1943.
G. van Noort, *De Ecclesia Christi,* Hilversum, 1932.
L. Walker, S.J., *The Problem of Reunion,* London, 1920.
Maisie Ward, *Insurrection versus Resurrection,* London, 1938.

d)   OTHER WORKS :

C. J. Cadoux, *Catholicism and Christianity,* London, 1928.
D. J. Dallin, *The Real Soviet Russia,* Yale, 1944.
F. Gavin, *Some Aspects of Contemporary Greek Orthodox Thought,* S.P.C.K., 1923.
W. A. Visser t'Hooft, *Anglo-Catholicism and Orthodoxy : A Protestant View,* London, 1933.
W. M. Horton, *Contemporary English Theology,* New York, 1936.
D. T. Jenkins, *The Nature of Catholicity,* London, 1942.
C. E. M. Joad, *The Present and Future of Religion,* London, 1930.
G. Johnston, *The Doctrine of the Church in the New Testament,* Cambridge, 1943.
Hugh Martin, *Towards Reunion,* London, 1937 (2nd ed.)
J. E. L. Newbigin, *The Reunion of the Church,* London, 1948.
E. Rosenstock-Huessy, *The Christian Future,* London, 1947.
R. Rouse and S. C. Neill, *A History of the Ecumenical Movement,* London, 1954.
George Salmon, *The Infallibility of the Church,* London, 1899.
George Slosser, *Christian Unity : its History and Challenge,* London, 1929.
T. O. Wedel, *The Coming Great Church,* London, 1947.

e)   ARTICLES IN PERIODICALS, ETC.

In the *Irish Ecclesiastical Record* :
Rev. W. J. Hegarty, 'The Latest Crisis in Anglicanism : The South India Scheme', *I.E.R.,* 5th series, vol. lxx, no. I (Jan. 1948), p. I ff.
Rev. G. Mitchell, 'Doctrine in the Church of England', *I.E.R.,* 5th. series, vol. li, no. 4. (April 1938), p. 337 ff.
'The Encyclical "Mystici Corporis Christi" ', *I.E.R.,* 5th. series, vol. lxii, no. 4 (April 1944), p. 217 ff.
'The Protestant Churches and Reunion', *I.E.R.,* 5th. series, vol. lvii, no. 4 (pril 1941), p. 327 ff.

In *Theological Studies* :
J. L. Monks, S.J., 'The Orthodox Churches on Anglican Orders',
            vol. x, no. I (March 1949), pp. 65-6.
In the *Dictionnaire de théologie catholique* (*D.T.C.*, 1903 ff) :
A. Gatard, 'Anglicanisme'.   (Useful only to the year 1900).   E.
Dublanchy, 'Église'.
In the *Catholic Encyclopaedia*, (1909) :
C. J. Callan, O.P., 'Unity'.
S. F. Smith, 'Union of Christendom'.

Where references are made to newspapers, sufficient details are
given in the footnotes.